PRAYERS FOR
ALL OCCASIONS

For Pastors and Lay Leaders

PRAYERS FOR ALL OCCASIONS

ROY PEARSON

Judson Press®   Valley Forge

PRAYERS FOR ALL OCCASIONS
Copyright © 1990
Judson Press, Valley Forge, PA 19482-0851

Second Printing, 1992

Library of Congress Cataloging-in-Publication Data
Pearson, Roy, 1914–
    Prayers for all occasions : for pastors and lay leaders / Roy Pearson.
      p. cm.
    ISBN 0–8170–1127–7
    1. Prayers.   I. Title.
    BV245.P36   1990   90–33642
    264'.13—dc20   CIP

With gratitude to the
New Hampshire churches
of my latter-day interim ministries,
where most of these prayers
were first offered:

Union Congregational Church, Peterborough
United Church of Christ, Newport
First Baptist Church, New London
Church of Christ at Dartmouth College, Hanover
United Church, Warner
First Congregational Church, Hopkinton

*here were priests in
the priesthood of all believers*

CONTENTS

CONTENTS

CONTENTS

PREFACE

Although nothing prevents the use of this book in private devotion, it is intended primarily as an aid to ministers in their leadership of corporate worship. Most members of the clergy are already supplied with volumes of prayers compiled for similar usage, and the warrant for still another includes the unsettling rapidity with which a church's regular worship consumes such resources, the advantages of wide choice in matching prayers with particular needs, and the endless demand for updating in language and reference. This book is designed not to replace but to supplement the prayers contained in other collections, not to stifle but to quicken a pastor's own creativity, not to impose prayers forever inviolate but to provide texts inviting addition and subtraction.

Some of the prayers may be found suitable in parts of a service other than those here suggested. A few invocations, for example, may be thought long enough to be short pastoral prayers, and portions of some pastoral prayers may serve as invocations. The provision for special occasions is inescapably partial, but there are prayers for the church year and for other notable days commonly regarded as having religious significance. With the exception of biblical phrases long since incorporated into ordinary speech and other odd groupings of words that may have been dredged unidentified from the fathomless depths of memory, everything in the prayers is new and original. It is assumed that most ministers will read the prayers substantially as printed, and this expectation has influenced the selection of words and continuity of phrases and sentences. The planned coursings, alternations, and rhythms are doubtless more apparent to their author than to anyone else, but the effect of the reading will be enhanced by two or three dry runs before the presentation in public.

I confess to lingering discontent in abandoning the long-accustomed pronouns of deity. Blithely ignoring their common-speech origins, I have found their anachronism a reverential distinction when referring to God; and partly from habit and partly from stubborn resistance to the rather sudden alteration of common practice in the matter, I have until recently preserved unchanged the thou-thee-and-thine mode with which I began my ministry more than fifty years ago. At long last, however, I have hazarded the great leap, and prompted, I am sure, by the desire to prove myself less than entirely superannuated, I have increased the possibility that the book will be published and used by preparing all of the prayers with the you-and-your pronouns. But I still cannot wholly avoid guilt in my presumption and brashness, and again and again I have prayed as I wrote: "Forgive me, O Lord, for calling thee you."

There have been comparable problems with reference to gender, and I have not been able fully to solve them. Wherever possible, I have tried to evade them by linguistic ingenuity, but sometimes I could discover no route of escape without indulging in clumsiness to which I did not want to subject the thought. Recent studies in the Lord's Prayer have indicated that "Father" is the only word surely attributable to Jesus' own authorship, and I have made large use of it in these prayers. Any who prefer other designations should have little difficulty adopting them. In other instances where gender explicit nouns and pronouns were seemingly inevitable, I have compromised by sometimes awarding precedence to the feminine and sometimes to the male.

INTRODUCTION

It is a reminder, apparently needless but often essential, that the point of convergence in worship is God. As William Temple has written: "To worship is to quicken the conscience by the holiness of God, to feed the mind with the truth of God, to purge the imagination by the beauty of God, to open the heart to the love of God, to devote the will to the purpose of God."

In actual practice the decision to attend a church service may be made after promptings many and varied: following habit; assuaging boredom or conscience; showing support for the institution or being edified and instructed; meeting friends or impressing neighbors; collecting gossip or setting an example for children. As subordinate interests these incentives are scarcely heinous, but the overriding purpose of worship is the ascription of worth to God, conceived as a being prepared to communicate. The dangers implicit in this assertion are obvious and include arrogance, self-deception, anthropomorphism, and oversimplification; but unless worship abandons its warrant in farce, it is neither pretext of fact nor pretense of truth, not play-acting and not autosuggestion. It is commerce with the almighty God and eternal Spirit who comprehends and responds.

A complete order of service contains all of the classic components: awareness, adoration, thanksgiving, penitence, forgiveness, intercession, petition, and the commitment involved in dedication and trust. Not every service will follow exactly this sequence, and the separate steps can be variously assigned in the constituent segments; but always the focus is God.

For the most part, worship flows in two directions, both of them vertical. On the one hand, the creatures address their Creator as they speak to God through the offering, prayers, affirmations, and some hymns, anthems, and solos. On the other hand, the Creator responds to these creatures by speaking

to them through assurances of pardon, Scripture, sermon, benediction, and some calls to worship. Once in a while the movement is horizontal, from creature to creature, as in some calls
to worship and parts of some hymns like *O Worship the King,
Fight the Good Fight,* and *Stand Up, Stand Up for Jesus.*
Usually, however, these occurrences are parentheses in the
progression of the service and merit only limited usage.

A worshiping congregation is more than a congregation of
worshipers. Corporate worship is not a public assembly of in-
dividuals praying privately. Where two or three are gathered
together in Christ's name, something happens that could not
take place were the two or three to return to their homes and
pray by themselves, and the familiar comparison with a symphony orchestra is quite apt. The leader is the conductor and
the worshipers the musicians, but what if the conducted refuse
the conductor's conduction? With consummate skill he waves
his arms before them, but the pianist's hands never touch the
keys, and the clarinets are never raised to the lips, and the
drummer's sticks never beat on the drums. Public worship suc-
ceeds or fails in direct conjunction with the participation of the
worshipers, and when all of the trumpets are playing, and all
of the violins, bass viols, and cymbals, a congregation is much
more than the sum of its parts.

Questions sometimes arise about the demonstrable efficacy
of the prayers we offer in worship, and the answer always lies
in the relation of power to purpose. An airplane is powerful, but
not for binding a book; a hammer is powerful, but not for
threading a needle; a bulldozer is powerful, but not for soothing
a baby. So with prayer, and when our prayers are assessed for
their communication of ideas, feelings, and petitions to God,
it may reasonably be assumed that their power is sufficient for
their purpose. To a not inconsiderable degree, their success will
depend on how well the pastor has discerned the mind of the
congregation for which the prayers are being offered, how well
its needs are interpreted, summarized, and expressed. To some
extent, too, the effect of the prayers will depend on how fully
the congregation enters into the praying, how faithfully the
worshipers supplement the minister's generalities with their

own particulars. But if God exists and is Christlike, there is small cause for doubt that the prayers are heard and comprehended.

Too much weight is frequently given to the significance of prayer in affecting God's action, and we need above all to avoid the reverse expectation of the Kodak advertisement: "You press the button, and we'll do the rest." In public as well as in private, much of our praying is not aimed at changing God's mind. Adoration and praise, confession and commitment seek not to alter God's decisions but to acknowledge God's acts. At some traffic lights I have noticed the sign that says "Delayed Signal," and do we not often become impatient when the answers to our prayers are delayed? A minister prays for five minutes, says "Amen," and announces the offering. How can God respond when we have allotted so little time? Sometimes prayer is like a planted seed, requiring months or years for its blossoms and fruit; sometimes like the doctor's medications, not effecting their cure until we have despaired of their curing. Sometimes the help is not subsequent but coincidental, not after the praying but in it—like singers presenting the *Messiah*, transforming the hearers and transformed themselves in the singing.

Then there are those who tell of results direct and immediate. John Knox, for example, when interrupted in prayer at midnight and urged to rest from the long agony of his intercession for Scotland, angrily replied that his prayers had already won half of the country and, if he had not been distracted, would have taken the rest by daybreak. Mary Queen of Scots declared that she feared Knox's prayers more than all the armies of Europe! And for anyone who prays there is the encouraging fact that prayer presents God with a new situation and hence with fresh alternatives. "When I pray," writes L. Harold de Wolf, "I change the situation with which God has to deal. As far as certain specific events are concerned, what was the best he could do for me or for my friends before I prayed may still be the best now in this changed situation. But it may not."

Among the many misconceptions about corporate worship is

the dogma that in the priesthood of all believers everyone can approach God without intermediary. So we can, but this is not the central intent of the teaching. What is meant by the doctrine is that everyone has power and duty to be priest to one's neighbor, and this is one of the justifications of corporate worship. We need one another's ministry, and simply by our presence in the congregation we assist our sisters and brothers in their movement toward God.

Another misconception is that awareness of the awe and the majesty, the power and the love and the will of God is likely in worship without preparation. Too soon we scorn the trivial immensities of no heat and hard seating, unceasing chatter and mindless gossip, coming and going and dropping and bumping. Too brazenly we make no attempt to be ready ourselves: staying up late on Saturday night, oversleeping, gulping breakfast, barking at children, growling at spouses, stumbling into church with a crop of new ulcers, fretting about the roast in the oven and the car to be washed. What are we doing in church this morning? We don't really know; all we want is to go home.

There is misconceiving, too, when the claim is advanced by church members that they avoid the worship services because they get nothing out of them. Ministers would not be happy if most of the time their parishioners did not feel stronger, better and cleaner, more hopeful and more faithful when they went out of the church than when they came in; but as I have already suggested, the purpose of worship is not to receive but to give. It is often more desirable that worshipers go home fretful than contented, perplexed than satisfied, eager to produce than at ease with consuming. And many who say that they came to church to find God but left without success have reached a false conclusion. It is not uncommon to find but not recognize or to recognize but deny, lest affirming, we be confronted with unacceptable consequences.

Precisely determining excellence in worship is a difficult and perhaps impossible undertaking. I have participated in services strictly following the rules expounded in the most scholarly textbooks but revealing two minutes after the prelude that the worship was stillborn. I have also taken part in services that

broke all the rules and shattered all standards but from beginning to end lifted the heart into joy and compassion, opened
the mind to new light and new truth, and cleansed the soul of
its vice and its sin. God's wonders are still performed with
mysterious grace, and what matters at last is less that we hasten
God's progress than that we get out of God's way.

PRAYERS IN THE VESTRY

Our worship of you is about to begin, our Father. When we speak, let it be your word. When we sing, let it be to your praise. When we pray, let it be to do your will.

Lead us, O God, that we may be leaders of this people. Bring us to you that we may bring others. Cleanse us, enlighten us, empower us.

Lord, a congregation waits for our ministry, and we would lead its members in their worship. Help us no less to worship you ourselves. Save us from such preoccupation with means that we forget the end toward which we strive.

Let the hour that lies ahead of us be rich in opportunity for those who wait to worship you, our Father, and vouchsafe that we whose task it is to be their leaders lead them into faith and hope, righteousness and mercy, courage and love.

Help us, Lord, not to treat lightly the holy things soon to be placed in our keeping. Those who have come to this place for their worship have come with their faith and their hopes, their guilt and their fears, their commitments and their aspirations. Their hearts bleed easily. Lead us to heal and encourage. Teach us to strengthen and renew.

Lord, how hard it is to do as we ought! We know the good but choose the bad, admire the true but succumb to the false, want to be pure—but not yet. As we are ourselves, so must, too, this people be, and we pray that you will so move through us about to lead them in their worship that we may not only declare to them the wonderful works of your love but also enable them to become in all fulness faithful disciples of your Son, Jesus Christ.

We come to sing your praise, our Father. We come to speak your word. Help us so to speak and so to sing that we beckon this people toward your love and service.

Lord, today we have come to church, but more, we have come in quest of yourself. So prepare us, we pray, that we may enter your holy presence in reverence and gladness and that the service we render you in song and spoken word may be acceptable in your sight.

Our Father and our God, who have given us minds to know you, hearts to love you, and voices to declare your wonderful goodness, imbue us with grace at this time so to nourish this congregation in its worship that going forth at last, it may go as your people indeed—a royal priesthood, a holy nation.

God of all goodness and grace, Lord of all power and love, we come not to amuse or entertain or impress. We come not to parade our learning or display our talents or occupy prominent seats in your temple. We come instead to worship and to be of service to others who, too, have come to worship. Make us then channels for your spirit, voices for your word.

Almighty God, Holy Spirit, Creator, Sustainer, and Redeemer, before the service begins, we offer ourselves here to be ministers of your powerful grace. We are not good enough to serve your holy purposes—not strong enough, not wise enough, not pure enough. Yet all that is possible is possible for you, and we pray that you will so perfect our imperfections that for this congregation waiting now to worship you we become the carriers of your grandeur, the heralds of your righteousness, the enfleshment of your love.

Lord God of all peoples and nations, from a worldly world we approach a world in part otherworldly, and to this congregation we would stand for you as ushers bidding the pilgrims welcome and helping them to find a happy home for their souls in heavenly places. So easy it is for your human creatures to forget their more than human origins, and we pray that in the service about to begin we may so lift the hearts of this people that they may know themselves in truth to be your sons and daughters, born in time and destined for the timeless.

If we cannot help you in this service, Lord, at least let us not get in your way. Save us from being noisy when we ought to be quiet, silent when we ought to be singing, moving when we need to be still, lethargic when all the wonders of your love are being laid before us. Keep us from attracting attention to ourselves. Persuade us to point the way to you.

A moment will pass, our Father, and we shall be leading this congregation in its worship. Who waits there now in expectation of our ministry? Are there joys to be celebrated? Does someone mourn a child, a wife, a husband? Is a marriage broken, a job lost, a confidence betrayed? Let nothing we do dim hopes already flickering, savage wounds already bleeding, increase guilt for sins already repented. Prepare us to bring good news. Make us bearers of faith and courage.

Setting out to guide our people in their worship, we pray, our Father, that you will save us from setting out in the wrong direction. We seek not most to offer ways of meeting friends and neighbors, not most to produce fine music, sound instruction, thoughts of comfort, peace, and happiness. Before all else, and through and after, we would lift this congregation to such awareness of yourself that it needs no other refuge and owns no other lord. Disciples of your Son, our brothers and sisters have gathered here pledged to worship you in his name. Help us to hold them to their good intentions.

We need not tell you how imperfect we are, our Father. Better far than ourselves are countless men and women who could do far better the deeds that we are charged to do in this service. Still the tasks have been laid in our care, and we pray that you will do through us the works for which alone we are not able. It is your word we would speak, your praise sing, your love declare.

Lord, the world is yours and all its peoples. There is no place where we could not find you and nothing that does not bear the mark of your creation. Yet in this house of prayer we are gathered now in special hope of being near you, and we pray that we may kindle in this congregation an expectancy of your presence. Help us to open minds that they may discern you. Teach us to prepare hearts that they may receive you.

Father of all, it is good that we can be here, that we can withdraw and be quiet, that we can stop and consider. But we withdraw that we may then move out with assurance, are quiet that then we may speak without folly. We stop to start with greater strength, consider in order that we may listen for second opinions. Enable us, we pray, to waken this congregation to the needs of all your human creatures, to stir in this people the will to serve you by serving the least of your children. Let our brothers and sisters hear in us a voice for hunger and pain, for loneliness and homelessness, for fear and guilt and despair.

PRAYERS OF INVOCATION

GENERAL PRAYERS

Eternal God, our heavenly Father, we have come to this house of prayer to affirm the faith already possessed, to seek a deeper understanding of you, and to pledge our lives to your service. Help us so to speak and so to hear, so to think and so to pray that our hungers may be satisfied and our promises kept. Through Jesus Christ our Lord. *Amen.*

Father of might and of mercy, if we have sinned, chasten us; if we are ignorant, enlighten us; if we are weak, sustain us; if we are lonely, comfort us. Prevent us from thinking that the words spoken in this service will exhaust all that you have to say to us. Keep us ever open to the truth that is yet to be told. Through Jesus Christ our Lord. *Amen.*

Almighty and eternal God, who being homeless are everywhere at home and who loving each of your children as if it were your only child, yet love all of your creatures as if you had no special love for any one of them, tarry now among us here. Let our hearts awhile be home to you, and help us so to respond to your love that we may work for peace and righteousness upon the earth. Guide us into humility. Lure us into quietness. Lead us into faith. Through Jesus Christ our Lord. *Amen.*

Eternal Spirit, in whom we live and move and have our being, keep us from the folly of thinking that we know you completely and from the sadness of assuming that you are too great to be known at all. Grant us such faith in you that we live in peace, both with what we know and with what we cannot know. Through Jesus Christ our Lord. *Amen.*

God of all wisdom and grace, high and lifted up yet ever hearing your people when they turn to you in prayer, hear now your people met before you in this holy place. Strengthen the weak and humble the strong. Guide the lost; bind up the wounded; and grant that going forth at the end of our worship, we may go as faithful disciples of your Son, Jesus Christ, in whose name we pray. *Amen.*

We would that your hand might be upon us, our Father, and yet we would not. That you should lay it tenderly upon our heads in commendation of our goodness we are willing; yea, more, we are eager. But what if you should find our sin too stark for tenderness? So we tremble in the half-light, too unsure about the aspect of your face to be either complacent in our petty achievements or faithful in our obvious duties. To study and to do what you have asked of us in Christ, we pledged ourselves long since as Christians, and we pray that you will keep us restless until we keep our pledges. If you can with gentleness persuade us to your service, be gentle, we beseech you; but if not, do what you must to save us from loving ourselves to very death. In Jesus' name. *Amen.*

God of all power and love—origin, support, and destiny of everything that was and is and evermore shall be, how can human minds comprehend your majesty, how dare human hearts approach your grandeur? Yet how can we ignore your bountiful goodness, how keep silent in the midst of your glory? Hear then our prayer as we come to this place to praise you, and so fill our frail souls with your pure and enlivening spirit that when we have finished the worship now beginning, we may go forth new creatures in your sight. Through Jesus Christ our Lord. *Amen.*

Almighty and eternal God, you have summoned us to be disciples of your Son, Jesus Christ. Grant that we who seek so frequently that others listen to us be not surprised that you should sometimes ask that we listen to you. Hold back the world awhile as we are gathered here, we pray, and softening its din and roar, lead us to hear again your ancient and abiding word, whose thunder is often a silence. In Jesus' name. *Amen.*

God of all time and space and of all beyond all space and time, we turn our little selves toward you, and from our tiny spot in your vast domain we seek the benediction of your grace. Our selves are often such burdens to carry—so heavy, so awkward, so elusive, so hated. Harsh when we want to be kind, cold when we long to be warm, false when we set out to be true, weak when most we need to be strong—we wander through your gift of days unsure whom we see in our mirrors, uncertain who we wish that we were. Help us, Lord, to get ourselves off the backs of our selves, to identify our selves and accept our selves, to find and lose and find again in strength unknown and joy and peace beyond even our hoping. From false pride set us loose; from greedy ambition shake us free; from fear of change release us. And grant that this day we fall no further into sin, neither pass unheard a call to your service. Through Jesus Christ our Lord. *Amen.*

Eternal God, heavenly Father, you have created us in your own image and seen us swiftly lose our likeness to yourself. We gather in this place of worship, half glad that we have come, half wishing we had not. There is so much to be done in our lives outside, and we do not want to waste our time with inactivity. There is so much to be heard and said, and said and heard, and heard and said again, and we are loathe to miss a single hearing or saying. Yet being loud, we long to be quiet; hasty, we yearn to be still; unlovely, we hunger for love; and ever at war with ourselves and our neighbors, we seek the peace that is ever beyond us. Face us with mirrors, Lord, until we see what you have made us, and then face us with windows until we see what you would make of us. Close our mouths and open our hearts. Close our mouths and open our ears. Close our mouths and move our hands and feet. Let us not linger overlong in the twilight of goodness—neither day nor night, neither hot nor cold, neither really good nor truly bad. Wake us up. Send us forth. In Jesus' name. *Amen.*

Whatever can be done you can do, our Father, and whatever can be known already you know. Weak, we lean on your power; ignorant, we beg you to teach us. Where we have fallen, lift us up; where we wander in error, lead us back to the truth. Enable us to be faithful disciples of your Son, Jesus Christ, in whose name we pray. *Amen.*

Fill us with your spirit, Lord: so often we appear to be empty. Gird us with your strength: so many days we seem to be help-less. We long to be whole and wholesome people, to be loving at home and at peace with our friends and our neighbors, to be engaged in a work which makes the world a better dwelling place for the next generation. Sometimes we think we succeed, sometimes fail; but always we need your firm and effectual presence. Enlighten us, we pray; sustain us; direct us. Through Jesus Christ our Lord. *Amen.*

Creator Spirit, who lived and moved and had your being before anything was or anyone existed, be manifest, we pray, in this service. Let not our worship mock the words we use to describe it. We would not pretend a presence when the presence is absent, and what does it profit us to enter your house if you are not at home? Be then among us here, and open our souls to your will. Touch us with your love; imbue us with your power; guide us with your light. In Jesus' name. *Amen.*

So much of us is elsewhere, Lord, while so little is here. Is not part of us back in the kitchen or down in the cellar, over in the garage or out on the lawn? How much of us is here in our praying and singing, our hearing and speaking, and how much out there in a meal to be cooked or a car to be washed, an appliance to be repaired or a hedge to be trimmed? Pull us together, our Father. Get us all in one place, and let this for these moments be it. For when we worship you, we would offer all of our minds and our hearts, all of our bodies and souls. Through Jesus Christ our Lord. *Amen.*

Not only to worship have we come to this church today, O Lord, but also to witness. We would not parade our faith before the world as if we thought ourselves better than those of other persuasion and practice, but neither would we conceal it nor fail to declare our belief in its truth and its power. We therefore present our bodies before you as a living sacrifice, meant to proclaim to any and all that we love you, that we have found in you our strength and refuge and that we have committed ourselves to serve you. Through Jesus Christ our Lord. *Amen.*

Eternal God, high, lifted up and perfect in all your ways, we have come to this place to worship, and yet we have not. Before ever we had left our homes, while still we were deciding whether to go to church or to stay in our beds, we confess to our shame that what loomed the largest among our reasons for coming was not singing the praise of our King and Creator but performing a duty or impressing the children, returning a book or conveying a message, being seen in the right place or completing a deal, being diverted or chatting with friends and collecting the gossip. Save us, we pray, from trivial purpose and inadequate motive. Attract attention to yourself. Lift up our eyes. Command our hearts. Through Jesus Christ our Lord. *Amen.*

God almighty, God eternal, more patient than the ages and wise both in hasting and waiting, save us from wasting our time by being too busy. Bury deeper the nerves that run flush with the surface. Remove the hair triggers that prompt us to fire before ready. Cancel the orders that command us to set off at once in opposing directions. Calm us, Lord. Quiet us. Silence us. In these moments of worship help us to watch and to listen, to consider and to plan; and grant that we may find in the end the strait gate and the narrow way that lead us to life worth our living. Through Jesus Christ our Lord. *Amen.*

How many worlds there are in this place, our Father. How many spheres distinct and untouching! Alone we come, together we sit, and alone we depart; and none knows wholly another, and all know little of each. Apprise our minds of the lives that surround us; open our hearts to their joys and their sorrows, their gains and their losses, their hopes and their fears; and vouchsafe that, one in creation, we may no less be one in love and commitment. In Jesus' name. *Amen.*

Everlasting Spirit, mighty in your love and loving in your might, who have called us to worship you in spirit and in truth, be with us now in presence known and bade welcome. Let not the ease with which we take your name upon our lips prevent our truly meeting you, and through the mysteries of your divine invention find ways, we pray, to bridge our moats and breech our walls until, face to face with you, we have no choice but that we hear and heed. Through Jesus Christ our Lord. *Amen.*

Let your Holy Spirit be among us here, O Lord. If minds be distraught, let them be calmed. If hearts be hurt, let them be healed. If souls be stained, let them be cleansed. And when we have received the good news of your love, let it not be our shame that we kept it only for ourselves. Through Jesus Christ our Lord. *Amen.*

Eternal Father, once flesh in Jesus Christ and ever coming to your creatures in the fullness of your grace, forgive us that we have come to you with so little of ourselves. So much of us is still in bondage to the deeds left behind us, and so much of us is leaping toward responsibilities lying ahead. Yet we pray that you will not disdain the will that led us to be here at all and that being yourself with us you will so direct our hearts and minds that we at last are none the less with you. In Jesus' name. *Amen.*

Mighty Spirit, heavenly Father, you know our frailties even better than we know them ourselves. We seek truth, and we strain after wisdom. Yet so often we misread our own motives, so frequently think that we know all when we really know nothing. Most commonly we seem to be most positive when most positively mistaken. Save us from doing the right thing for the wrong reasons. Save us, more, from doing the wrong thing for the right reasons. Engage our hearts in what we undertake, but do not disengage our minds: let fact be balanced by compassion and compassion by fact. Guard us against ending with bad answers because we began with poor questions. Grant us courage in our convictions, honesty in our decisions, and charity in judging those who disagree with us. And when the work of this hour is past and behind, so chasten our unruly tempers and so discipline our rampant wills that we close ranks, link arms, and move forward in the name of Jesus Christ our Lord. *Amen.*

God almighty, God eternal, in whom is all truth and all wisdom, help us so to worship you in truth that we may in truth be wise, and so shape our lives without error or folly that your will in us is done through Jesus Christ our Lord. *Amen.*

Spirit high and holy, not seen by the eye, unheard by the ear, imperceptible to taste or smell or touch, we long to find you, to encounter you, to meet you. Yet ever you surge ahead of us, and always we scramble behind you. We see what the doer has done but never the doer. Fleetingly now will you not reveal yourself? Will you not make yourself known? In Jesus' name. *Amen.*

God of grace, God of glory, God of mystery and wonder, who made what was and design what yet shall be, desert not those who live with what is. When the good die young and the wicked live long, when truth wavers and falsehood prevails, when cancer kills a baby and a drunk driver maims an innocent mother, when the poor are homeless and the rich turn away in selfishness, when war rages and famine spreads, when arsonists burn and terrorists bomb and drugs destroy—we struggle for answers, Lord. Will you not help us to find them? In these moments of worship will you not teach us to interpret your silences, to discover meaning in the meaningless, to find the road toward understanding and hope? Through Jesus Christ our Lord we pray. *Amen.*

God of all strength and all goodness, to whom none can compare in might nor in freedom from evil, so fill us with your spirit, we pray, that we may become heralds of your righteousness, agents of your love, bearers of your peace. Through Jesus Christ our Lord. *Amen.*

To whom shall we turn but to you, O Lord? In pain and anguish, in loss and betrayal, in vision clouded and hope deferred—to whom shall we turn but to you? Grant then that we may rest awhile in the arms of your love, and in your Holy Spirit find renewal and hope. Through Jesus Christ our Lord. *Amen.*

Almighty and eternal God, Creator of all the worlds that are and of all that is in them, shall we call you Father or Mother? As a father you have begotten us and as a mother you have borne us. With strength like a father's you defend us from harm, and in a mother's tenderness you heal and restore us. Save us from stopping too soon when we set out to find you. Are you not high and lifted up? Must we not seek you beyond all human distinctions? In Jesus' name. *Amen.*

Eternal God, omnipotent, omniscient, and abounding in love for your people, be not angry when we try to change your mind, temper your decisions, direct your ways. Be not angry, but neither be obeisant. When we do not pray as we ought, answer as we need. Through Jesus Christ our Lord. *Amen.*

Holy Spirit, Creator, Lord and Redeemer: let everything done here be done as in your sight. When we speak, help us to speak your word. When we hear, open our ears to your teaching. When we sing, we would sing to your praise. When we give, we would make our offerings as if to yourself. For yours is the kingdom and the power and the glory; world without end. *Amen.*

How far we are from the nearest to us, Lord, and how vastly farther from the farthest! We know so little about those we know best, and about so many others we know nothing at all. Keep us aware of our brothers and sisters, we pray, and let none of your children appear not as a sister or a brother. Through Jesus Christ our Lord. *Amen.*

Eternal God and merciful Father, in whose name this house of prayer was raised and to whom we come when we enter to worship, it is good for us to be here, but not for too long. We assemble for rest and renewal. We gather to be lifted up and set down redirected. But is not our mission outward, Lord? Is not our task to get out of the church and get the church out? Do you not need us out in the world among your people in need? Empower us to be your ministers, we pray, and at the end of our worship put us to work. Through Jesus Christ our Lord. *Amen.*

God almighty, God eternal, you have brought us to being in a world beyond our comprehension. Save us from the trivial. Give us no peace in the puny. Keep us restless in the trifling, the idle, the petty. Beckon us to high mountains; lure us to deep waters. Speak to us of heavy burdens; tell us of rough crosses. You have called us to yourself, and small though we are, we would feed on your greatness. Through Jesus Christ our Lord. *Amen.*

Everlasting God and heavenly Father, through ages past you have summoned apostles and teachers to serve you and through them have taught us that we are your chosen people. Spare us the pretense of teachers' pets. Chosen for obedience, we have enlisted for labor. Take us at our word, Lord. Take us at our word. In Jesus' name. *Amen.*

Merciful Father, in each of whose children there is nothing unseen by you and nothing unknown, help us to cast off, to shed, to discard. Peel away the many skins of our worries and fears, our jealousies and hatreds, our obligations and duties. Show us ourselves as you designed us to be; and bowed and repentant, but cleansed and forgiven, may we rise up to run the race that you have set before us. Through Jesus Christ our Lord. *Amen.*

We have come to this holy place, our Father, and we wanted to come. Yet we would not let its walls imprison us. Our hearts reach out to all the world, and back with them they bring to you the hungry and homeless, the guilty and frightened, the bereaved and dying, the unemployed and despairing. Hear now the prayer we raise for them, and by any means at your command find ways, we beseech you, to feed, heal, defend, forgive, comfort, encourage. For we pray in Jesus' name. *Amen.*

Heavenly Father, who gave us life in the beginning and uphold us still by your spirit today, we offer you here our minds and our hearts, our souls and our bodies to be used by you in your will for the world. Cleanse, quicken, and direct them, we pray; and when you have need of our pledges, persuade us that we honor them. In Jesus' name. *Amen.*

God almighty, God eternal, clean, pure, unspotted and holy, we confess to you that we are not holy, not unspotted, pure or clean. We have sinned. Being and not being, doing and not doing, saying and not saying—we have stained our souls with offenses against yourself, and we are not worthy to be called your children. Yet still we return to our Father's house, cast ourselves at your feet and ask that you put us to work among your hired servants. Forgive us, we pray; save us; redeem us. Through Jesus Christ our Lord. *Amen.*

Day's end, our Father. We enter your house, and as often we have sought you in times that are gone, so now we seek you again. God of light, help us to see in the dark. So much of our life appears to be lived in the shadows—yearning in vain to perceive, to understand, to know without doubt or suspense. Shine your bright sun, we pray, where only pale stars have been. Confront, meet, reveal. In Jesus' name. *Amen.*

Dawn comes, our Father. We enter your house, and as often we have sought you in times that are gone, so now we seek you again. God of mercy, help us to see while yet there is light. So much of our life is spent after the fact—half of the day at end before we are even aware it had a beginning. Shock us early with your presence, we pray. Confront, meet, reveal. In Jesus' name. *Amen.*

Noon, our Father. We enter your house, and as often we have sought you in times that are gone, so now we seek you again. God of all brilliance and glory, illumine our hearts, we pray. One half of the day lies behind us, and we hunger to discover its meaning; the other half of the day is ahead, and we long to carry forward the meaning discovered. Teach us and show us, good Lord. Confront, meet, reveal. In Jesus' name. *Amen.*

Eternal God, majestic in power and grace, incomparable in grandeur and glory, we have come to this house of prayer to worship. Save us from becoming an audience: enduring in silence the time here committed, expecting the choir to soothe and delight us, daring the pastor to inform and inspire us, demanding dramatics to divert and amuse us. We would march with the soldiers, play in the orchestra, sing in the chorus, have a place on the team. So we pray that you will waken our minds, stir our hearts, fire our souls, and when the time comes to sing or to pray, open our mouths. Through Jesus Christ our Lord. *Amen.*

Everlasting God, Creator and Source of everything that was or now is, we would not be parasites even upon yourself, on whom we must feed for all that we have and all that we are. You have called us in the church to be a body for you on the earth, and when we try to lay on you the burdens that only your body can bear, return them, we pray, to ourselves. Compel us more often to think with our own minds, to love with our own hearts, to stand on our own feet, to work with our own hands. We would share with you the yoke of your purpose, and we would carry some of the weight on our own shoulders. Through Jesus Christ our Lord. *Amen.*

Almighty and eternal God, by whose providence the alternation of the day and the night is ordained, as the night descends and the shadows of evening steal over the land, spread abroad in our hearts your heavenly peace. Banish from our remembrance every unruly thought and unworthy affection. Silence the clamor of guilt and temptation, of worry and fear, of hatred and envy. Help us to forgive and forget, to count the day's evil enough for the day, to nurture no grudges beyond the day's end. Prepare us here for the sleep yet to come; in sleep bring us rest and renewal; and at breaking of dawn may we so break with past days that we rise up in strength and go forth in hope. Through Jesus Christ our Lord. *Amen.*

O God, whose power never fails and whose might never wavers, but who still rested at last from your labors in creation and who ordained a day too when your children could withdraw from their toil, forgive us when sometimes we seek in our worship an occasion less to advance than retreat. The world is often too much with us. In its getting and spending we lay waste our powers, and we need to restore them. Accept us though weak, we pray, receive us though weary. Restless with our many incapacities, may we find in you the rest that renews our strength. Through Jesus Christ our Lord. *Amen.*

Almighty God, eternal Father, who created all of earth's peoples, who loved and still love and hold them in your timeless care, be present in this sacred place, and so manifest yourself to this congregation that those who ask receive and those who seek find and to those who knock the door is opened. Through Jesus Christ our Lord. *Amen.*

21

O God, truthful, just, and righteous altogether, by your prophets of old we have been warned of judgment in the final days. Judge us, we pray, while time still remains for repentance. Be a mirror to us in the moments here and now to be spent, and shaming us with what we see, forgive us and cleanse us, renew us and save us. In Jesus' name. *Amen.*

Forgive us, O Lord, the low expectations with which we have entered your house today. Often we have come, and nothing appears to have happened. We have behaved ourselves with decorum; we have departed politely; and all at the end is unchanged from all at the start. Break us, we pray, of bad habits. Help us to look and to listen, to wait and to wonder, to seek and to search. Will it be now that a candle illumines our darkness? Will it be here that a still voice speaks in our silence? In Jesus' name. *Amen.*

Almighty and everlasting God, everywhere present and always at home, we call your name, not to ask that you come, but to pray that you bless. If any words spoken here or deeds done here are found acceptable in your sight, so empower and enable them, we beseech you, that they may be tools of your purpose. Through Jesus Christ our Lord. *Amen.*

Eternal God—Creator, King, and Redeemer—you call your people to come to you in spirit and in truth; we sanctify ourselves for the sake of our sisters and brothers. If we cannot help them in their worship, we would not hurt. Keep us from disrupting their prayers by irrelevant talk and extraneous movement. Save us from inserting ourselves between you and your people. Make us transparent, and looking toward us, may our brothers and sisters see through us to you. In Jesus' name. *Amen.*

Be here our Teacher, O Lord, and teach us at least a sense of proportion. If we must be troubled, let it be by matters big enough to warrant the trouble. Keep us from rolling out a cannon to shoot down a fly. Lift up our minds to high mountains. Send out our hearts to far horizons. Through Jesus Christ our Lord. *Amen.*

O God, you who love all of your children with a love surpassing our knowledge, we confess that we have often been paltry and vengeful, cankered, embittered, and sour. Nullify the acid within us, we pray. Sweeten our juices. Feed us with kindness and pity, with forbearance and peace, with courage and hope. Let worship's end be life's new beginning. Through Jesus Christ our Lord. *Amen.*

SPECIAL OCCASIONS

Advent and Christmas

How long you waited, our Father! How long you waited before you moved in the void and out of the emptiness created the heavens and the earth! How long you waited before you breathed on earth's dust and brought to their being the souls of your children, and how much longer before you gave them the Son you loved! Still today we wait for him: we wait for him as those who watch for the morning. Prepare us, we pray. Make us ready. For we pray in his name. *Amen.*

God of ages swiftly passing and of times never ending, as the day nears when we celebrate the birth of your Son, help us to prepare a way for his coming, to make straight in earth's deserts a highway for your purpose. We would act justly and love mercifully and walk humbly. We would deny ourselves and lay down our lives and take up our crosses. In Jesus' name. *Amen.*

Almighty and eternal God, whom no eye has ever seen nor ear heard speak a word, we await the coming of your Son; save us from looking for him in the wrong places. Will he, born once in a manger, choose now a palace for his new appearing? Will he, heard gladly by the dispossessed, be found today among the mighty? Lead us in the paths of the humble; nudge us toward the homes of the lowly. Keep us close to the ground in our searching. Sink us to our hands and our knees. In Jesus' name. *Amen.*

Holy Spirit, acquainted no less with the dark than the light, as fully with the bad as the good, forgive us our trifling with Christmas. Disturb the ease with which we hail the Christ born in a manger but forget altogether the manger's surroundings— the brutal wars and the savage rebellions; the pampered rich and the tortured poor; the starving and the homeless; the lonely and the sick and the dying. Lead us beyond the tinsel, Lord. Give us no rest until we come to the cross on the darkened hill and the empty tomb in Joseph's garden. Through Jesus Christ our Lord. *Amen.*

Almighty God, everlasting in time and eternal in being, glory to you in the highest. On earth let there be peace among those with whom you are pleased, and number us here with the builders and makers. Beget in us enobling aspirations; kindle in us healing resolutions; nurture in us kindly virtues. Purge us of hatred. Imbue us with love. Through Jesus Christ our Lord. *Amen.*

Almighty God, eternal Spirit, bearing good tidings of great joy to all of your people, build anew in our hearts the City of David, and again let your Son be born on the earth. Open our doors in hope of his advent, and finding before us a man betrayed or a woman distraught or a child abused and abandoned, may we not fail to recognize the One whom we see. In Jesus' name. *Amen.*

So much truth we hear in the Christmastide, our Father; so much beauty we see; so much love we signalize and celebrate. Move us to keep these things. Move us to keep these things through all the coming days and to ponder them in our hearts. Through Jesus Christ our Lord. *Amen.*

25

Everlasting God, who long ago watched as the wise men followed a star and found a manger, we turn from the manger in search of the star. Renew our faith in the importance of the humble, the power of the meek, the significance of the insignificant, the origin of earthly things in heavenly purposes. Creator of all things and all people, let us not behold the works of your hands and forget the hands of the Worker. In Jesus' name. *Amen.*

New Year's Day

Eternal God, in whose sight a thousand years are but as yesterday when it is past, bless to us our use of this day. Sufficient unto the year is the evil thereof, and to that year just ended we return the encumbrances it crushed upon us: the paltry fears and petty envies, the strutting pride and vaunted puffing, the greedy scrambling and surly resenting, the evil thoughts and hateful deeds. Gladly, our Father, we surrender its wretchedness to the times that contained it, and the year thus burdened we cast to the void of vanished remembrance. Unfettered and free, we offer ourselves to you for your shaping. Take us, we pray, and in the new year that opens before us, keep the old from ever again exerting dominion. Make us new. Through Jesus Christ our Lord. *Amen.*

God of all ages, Lord of every time, we stand on the line where the two years meet, and as the bells ring out the old and in the new, we lift up our eyes to the hills whence comes our help. Above the din and tumult of those who make merry, attune our ears to the sounds of the silences, to whispers heard only by souls, to still small voices mocking with their quiet might the fury of earthquake and wind and fire. It is you whom we seek, our Father, you we love and you we long to serve. Forgive us our sins as we forgive those who sin against us. Lead us not into further temptation. And yours be the kingdom and the power and the glory forever. *Amen.*

Everlasting God, you who command the times in their courses and govern the centuries in their going and coming, we begin the year in hope. Grant that we run its race with faithfulness and attain its end without shame. Through joy or through sorrow, in strife or in peace, by loss or by gain, teach us the meaning of this earthly life, and let us so be profited by your wisdom and grace that taught the good, we do it. Through Jesus Christ our Lord. *Amen.*

27

Epiphany

Eternal Father, most glorious and most gracious, who created the earth and ordained that all of its people be disciples of your Son, claim us for your purpose. Aid us so to worship you that our hearts may be warmed by your love and our lives laid before you as offerings on your altar. Make us allies of your justice, ushers of your compassion, builders of your peace. Through Jesus Christ our Lord. *Amen.*

God of all nations and peoples, who first revealed your Son to the Gentiles when wise men followed the star to the manger, keep us restless while camels still find it easier to go through the eye of a needle than the rich to enter the kingdom of heaven. Divest us, we pray, of anything which blocks us from yourself: whether money or lands, whether pride or ambition, whether comfort or sloth. Cause us to be again as little children, moving toward you with eyes unmisted by our own corruptions and kneeling at last as with the kings from far countries, where your might is proclaimed in the birth of a baby. In Jesus' name. *Amen.*

Almighty and eternal God, we are disciples; help us to make disciples, and save us from complacency when none but the poor and the humble have heard your Son gladly. As wise men of old sought the stable's manger, so now we covet the day when all the kingdoms of the world shall become the kingdom of your Son, Jesus Christ, and he shall reign for ever and ever. Help us to help the ones who think they need no help, and grant that kneeling in heart before the manger, the rich may find themselves poor and the poor rich, the strong weak and the weak strong, and all of them your children—brothers and sisters redeemed by your love. In Jesus' name. *Amen.*

Racial Justice Observances

God almighty, God eternal, from whom came all of earth's nations and peoples, we thank you for the incredible diversity of your creation. How wonderful the differences of color and shape and size. How marvelous the variance in opinion and insight and preference! Save us from thinking that you love some of your children better than others. Teach us to probe beneath the surface to the substance. Lead us to find the harmony uniting all divergences, and on the one earth, our one home, establish us, we pray, in one communion of peace and respect, excluding none of our brothers and sisters. Through Jesus Christ our Lord. *Amen.*

Almighty God—origin, ground, and destiny of earth and all it contains and supports—you have made of one blood all of earth's races, and we thank you for this people gathered here from many walks and ways. Apart, we long to be one; together, we rejoice in our diversity. You are the Father of all. Accept, then, the praise all offer you, and so discipline our wayward hearts that we bear upon ourselves the likeness of the One who made us. Through Jesus Christ our Lord. *Amen.*

Did your hand slip, our Father? Did you make a mistake? Had you planned that all of your children be white or black or all yellow or red or brown; and then did you lose the recipe and mismix the dyes as you struggled to regain the desired proportions? But if not, and if all remains as at first you intended the colors to be, how can we hate what you, our God and Creator, ordained? How, Lord? How? *Amen.*

Ash Wednesday

Almighty God, Holy Spirit, who watched with a father's eye while your Son did battle for his soul in the wilderness, abandon not your sons and daughters in their own temptations. Have we not a wilderness still to be faced and endured—the savagery and vengefulness, the tawdriness and emptiness, the despair and the greed, and the lust and the lying? Let not the chaos destroy us, Lord, and by our very wrestling with its harmful might, so increase our strength, we pray, that we run and grow not weary, that we walk and not faint. Through Jesus Christ our Lord. *Amen.*

Lead us not into temptation, our Father; for we confess that already we love our sinning. Steel us against all enticement to evil, and so attract us to the true and the good that we repent indeed of our sins and sin no more. In Jesus' name. *Amen.*

Holy God, in whom is no evil or wrong of any kind, you care for your people with love everlasting and offer forgiveness to all who truly repent of their sins. We confess that we have done wrong in your sight, broken your solemn laws, and turned from the road that leads to redemption. We knew the good but did the bad, knew the bad but scorned the good: we are without excuse. Be merciful to us, we pray. Again be merciful, and so fill our hearts with your pure strength that we stumble no more into wickedness but walk in the light to the end of our days on the earth. Through Jesus Christ our Lord. *Amen.*

Palm Sunday

God of our time and of all other times, we commemorate in your presence the hastening death of your Son, and we call to your special remembrance that day when he rode into the Holy City while multitudes shouted his praise and laid down their garments before him. Fill our own hearts with half of his courage, half of his faithfulness, honor, and wisdom. Comrades in his glory, we would no less be companions at his cross. For we pray in his name. *Amen.*

God of power and mercy, beyond all time yet marking each second of time as it passes, recall to our good the triumphant procession: the King on a donkey on his way to the cross. We would not trifle with that day, our Father, not trivialize, not prettify. Did not the crowds that waved their palms and cried hosanna raise quite soon their fists and shout to crucify? Let us not betray your Son in his assault on the city. Lift up our eyes to his grandeur. Bend our knees to his courage. *Amen.*

Sovereign God and mighty Father, you who come to us most commonly in humble and lowly ways, we give you thanks and praise that for the times of your surest revealing you chose a man who was born in a stable and who rode on a donkey. Like those of old who laid down their garments before him, we too would wave our palms and cry hosanna; but shield us from mistaking the King that we hail. Still keep it hard for the proud to enter the kingdom; still let the meek inherit the earth. Through Jesus Christ our Lord. *Amen.*

Maundy Thursday

Eternal Father, who so loved the world that you gave it your Son, revivify in our hearts the upper room. Show us again the ominous shadows. Surround us once more with the anxious hearkening and the frightening silences, the furtive whispering and the unsettling sounds through the door and the windows. Let us not take lightly the bread and the cup. Help us to find in them the body and the blood; and broaden our vision, deepen our faith. Through Jesus Christ our Lord. *Amen.*

Father of Jesus Christ and our Father, you who suffer with all who suffer and rejoice with them that rejoice, grant that we may be here indeed as in an upper room, above the din of the streets, apart from the pressure of abrading demands. Help us to think, and think clearly; stir us to feel, and feel deeply. Let our retreat be that of those who prepare to advance, our peace that of them who make ready for battle. Fill us with love of your kingdom and courage to work for its coming. Through Jesus Christ our Lord. *Amen.*

Almighty and eternal God, no event is unknown to you; you manifest yourself ever in particular. Be particularly among us, we pray, as we do this deed in the name of your Son. Let the bread be to us as the body and the cup as the blood; and receiving the seen, may we welcome the invisible presence of him who is host at our table. We would follow him, our Father; we would be like him. Enlarge our faith. Deepen our courage. *Amen.*

Good Friday

Holy God, merciful Father, you know our thoughts as we think them and hear our words before we speak. Hear nonetheless our prayer as we call to memory the crucifixion of our Lord Jesus Christ. How long ago it seems, how far away! Yet do not good men and women still suffer at the hands of the bad no farther from us than our daily rounds? Guard us against self-righteousness; defend us against complacency; save us from thinking ourselves incapable of wrongs we abhor in our brothers and sisters. Lord, we are able, and we plead for your disabling. In Jesus' name. *Amen.*

Creator God and everlasting Father, from whose family of earth no soul is cast out, let not this holy day fall behind us until we know the deeper meanings of the crucifixion. We praise your Son more ardently than we obey him; we are more readily Christian than Christlike; we wear the cross more often than we bear it. Is there any road to Joseph's garden that does not visit Calvary? If so, reveal it to us, Lord; but if not, let not the cup be taken from us. In Jesus' name. *Amen.*

Forgive us, our Father, for the sins by which we still hammer nails into the cross. Selfishness and arrogance and greed, jealousy and sloth and envy and hatred—of these and more we are guilty, and by these and more we raise again the cross on Golgotha's hill. We are without excuse or alibi. We know what we do, and when our Lord is crucified, we are there in presence undisputed. Be merciful to us, for without your mercy all our hope is hopeless. Forgive us our sins, and stop us from sinning. Forgive us, and save us. In Jesus' name. *Amen.*

Easter

Almighty God, eternal Father, who raised from the dead your Son and who conquers death in all who trust him, we celebrate in your holy presence the resurrection of our Lord Jesus Christ. From the thousand deaths of daily living we come to hail the life no death could kill, and we praise you for your power; we thank you for your love. Receive our worship, we pray, and so cleanse our minds and warm our hearts that we magnify your name in spirit and in truth. *Amen.*

Roll back again the stone from the door of the tomb, our Father. Set free the good intentions, the gallant aspirations, and the noble commitments so long held hostage by fear and self-seeking. Raise from the dead the lives that you gave us for living, and aid us to live them with faith born anew and hope undying. Through Jesus Christ our Lord. *Amen.*

Holy Spirit, ever near us though we do not see you, keep us from looking for Jesus where Jesus is not. Save us from tarrying too long in the place where the Lord lay. Was it not the angel's word that he had risen as he said? Drive us, then, soon out of the tomb, and let us depart quickly with fear and great joy. Teach us to spread the word, enable us to proclaim the glad tidings, help us to make disciples of all nations. In Jesus' name. *Amen.*

Creator of all worlds, Lord of all nations, Father of all peoples, we come to the tomb but leave it quickly; for Jesus is not here. Is he not where he always was—among the poor and the hungry, the lost and the homeless, the betrayed and the lonely? Send us to him, we pray. Lead us to him swiftly, for we pray in his name. *Amen.*

Family Sunday

Eternal Father, who created us male and female and ordained that we dwell together in families, we present our homes to you for your blessing. Forgive in them all lapses of trust and forbearance, all laxness in patience and caring, all failures in defending and helping. Grant that by our worship at this time we may be prepared to mend our past ways and, being truly repentant, walk no more where they led us. Through Jesus Christ our Lord. *Amen.*

Loving and compassionate God, who designed that we love and be loved in our homes, we hunger to be as you intended. Enable us therefore not to be jealous or boastful, not arrogant or rude, not irritable or resentful. Help us not to insist upon our own way, not to rejoice in wrong but rejoice in the right. Teach us to bear all things, believe all things, hope all things, endure all things. Through Jesus Christ our Lord. *Amen.*

God of all wisdom and knowledge, from whom no secrets are hid, give us the courage to see ourselves as the ones we love best have seen us, to hear ourselves as they have heard. Humble us with your mirrors. So often we smile at strangers and snarl at loved ones. We preen ourselves in public and live like tramps at home. We have time for our friends and business associates but none for our husbands, our wives, and our children. In our worship of you, make us aware of ourselves, O Lord. Lead us into penitence. Send us out new creatures. In Jesus' name. *Amen.*

Pentecost

God the Creator, God the Father, who brought us to being from the dust of the ground, you have no means but your creatures to work your will upon the earth. We pray for the church. Let it be indeed the body of your Son, and through the worship that we render you here, teach us to be fingers and eyes, to be ears and tongues. We would be a tool for him. We would be a voice. Hear us, we pray, for we pray in his name. *Amen.*

Not for the mighty wind do we pray, our Father, nor for the tongues of flame. Yet in humbler guise we ask that your Holy Spirit be in truth among us as we hail the church and its mission at home and abroad. Let it rouse us from languor, inspire us with faith, commit us to labor and fill us with hope. Make us in fact what already we claim to be: disciples of your Son, Jesus Christ, for we pray in his name. *Amen.*

We love the church, O Lord, and loving it, we pray that you will chasten it. Permit it no peace when peace is all it seeks. Prepare it for conflict. Post its marching orders. Summon it to battle. Engage it in strife with all that thwarts your holy purpose: deceit and injustice, cruelty and hatred, prejudice and torture, oppression and violence. Make it the comrade of all who bend the knee to your will: the upright and truthful, the loving and caring, the brave and the merciful, the honest and the faithful. Let the church not be confined by the buildings it has erected. Send it out; lead it out; drive it out. In Jesus' name. *Amen.*

Memorial Day

Lest we forget, our Father, induce us to remember. Recall to us the endless wars that never ended war, the promised peace that seldom was peaceful, the millions slaughtered in causes deceitfully labeled, the property destroyed by means irreversible, the dreams crushed, the hopes shattered. Make us makers of peace, lest forgetting what we need to remember, we do again the deeds we ought never to have done. Through Jesus Christ our Lord. *Amen.*

God of all nations and peoples, we hail today our own beloved homeland, conceived in liberty and dedicated to the proposition that all of your children were created by you to be equal. Compel us to make good on our pledges. Have no patience with proud declarations unsupported by appropriate institutions and actions. What we have preached, demand that we practice. Diligent in labor and faithful in duty, may we build in this place a bulwark for freedom, a stronghold for justice. Through Jesus Christ our Lord. *Amen.*

Almighty and eternal God, before whom nothing was, in whom all coheres, and from whom there is neither escape nor departure, we present for your blessing all who have fought the good fight, kept the faith, and finished their courses. Accept their labor, we pray, as done for your sake. Redeem their sacrifice, and let it accrue to the good of the dispossessed and the persecuted, the distraught and the lonely. Grant that though dead, they yet may live in our hearts. By our worship at this time, prepare us, we pray, to walk in their footsteps. Through Jesus Christ our Lord. *Amen.*

Children's Day

Almighty God, Creator of all things and Father of all people, we pray for our children. Rekindle in our minds an awareness of our duty to them. Remind us anew how deeply their growth and well-being depends upon the care with which we surround them. Are they not as ourselves: neither devils nor angels? Help us then to understand how best to guide and instruct them, and strengthen our will to be faithful. Through Jesus Christ our Lord. *Amen.*

O God, Creator, Lord and Redeemer, you who embrace in your holy love all the people whom you have begotten, hear us as we commend to your special concern the children of our homes, our church, and the whole world. Forgive us for the wrongs that we have done them: withholding our time, denying their needs, polluting their land and their air and their water, demanding allegiance to false values and standards, stealing their future by loading their shoulders with conflicts that we ought to have settled and debts that were ours to pay. For these and all things more of which we are guilty we ask your pardon, our Father, and we pray that through our worship here we may be cleansed of our sin and made ready to nurture our children in the fullness of love and commitment. In Jesus' name. *Amen.*

Father, Son, and Holy Spirit, who love our children with a love surpassing even our own, we confess that we are unworthy of the treasure that you placed in our hands at their birth. Cleanse our minds of error, we pray; purge our hearts of impatience and coldness; empty our souls of resentment and anger; and help us so to rejoice in sharing with you the shaping of the days yet to come, that our children find in us a pathway to yourself. In Jesus' name. *Amen.*

Independence Day

For all in past years who have labored for freedom with justice we lift up our hearts in praise of you, O God, by whose hand they were created and in whose love they were nurtured. Keep us ever mindful of the shoulders on which our present liberties were carried, and foster in us, we pray, the courage to offer our own backs for new burdens. Through Jesus Christ our Lord. *Amen.*

Deliver us, Lord, from being too free for our own good. Defend us against the liberties that do no more than make fools of their servants. Save us from the freedoms better labeled licenses to do evil. When we are emancipated, let it not be from honor and decency. Through Jesus Christ our Lord. *Amen.*

God of all lands and all peoples, we pray for our own nation. We celebrate in your presence its abundant achievements in freedom and justice for all, and we confess before you its many and grievous departures from matching deed with declaration. Confirm, we pray, the good bravely done; shame us with the evil still performed. So hold in our vision the bright glow of your hope for this beloved realm that we see more clearly the work yet to be done, and do it, to the end that your kingdom may come and your will be done on the earth. Through Jesus Christ our Lord. *Amen.*

Labor Day

Almighty God, you care for your people with a love neither bounded nor ending. Hear us as we pray for all who work. Wheresoever they may be—in schools or in stores, in airplanes or in ditches, at office desks or at kitchen sinks, let them commit themselves to labor for the benefit of their sisters and their brothers. Help them to shield their toil from uselessness and boredom, from acrimony, enslavement, and greedy ambition. May they love you with all of their beings and may they offer their own small skills in the wide and wonderful world to which you offered your Son, our Lord Jesus Christ. *Amen.*

Lord God, Creator of all that we are and of all that we know and do not, were there not easier ways to make the world? Were there no simpler means of bringing forth the beasts of the field and the birds of the air and the fish of the sea? Need it have taken so long to beget a man and a woman? How endlessly you toiled and still toil! Apparently there are no shortcuts in creation, no readymade kits for building worlds and their peoples. A worker yourself, teach us to work beside you, and be patient with us when we grow impatient. In Jesus' name. *Amen.*

Eternal God, caring for us in our worship but caring no less in our work, on this day of rest make us ready for the days of work. Aid us to be worthy of our employment and to perform with faithfulness the duties of the toil by which we earn our daily bread. Keep us from needless strife with our fellow workers, and lead us to work with our colleagues in helpfulness and peace. Show us the mountains we build with our molehills; shield us from motives no higher than self; withdraw us from labor that hurts and destroys; enliven our sympathy with those poorly paid or out of jobs; and ever maintain in our hearts the eagerness to respond in our work to your will and your summons. Through Jesus Christ our Lord. *Amen.*

Reformation Sunday

For all the saints who rest from their labors we thank you, Lord, and especially here for our forefathers—the Protestant reformers. As we follow them in time, so would we follow in faith and courage, in wisdom and commitment. Grant us strength for the task, we pray, and let us not stumble or waver. Through Jesus Christ our Lord. *Amen.*

Almighty God, Father of all humankind of whatever race or religion, we offer you particular thanks for the gallant souls from whom our Protestant faith derives. Priests in the priesthood of all believers, we would not neglect our priestly calling, and we pray that you will keep us ever mindful of the duty we bear toward our sisters and brothers. Help us to be helpful, to be channels of grace between yourself and your people, and to claim for ourselves no blessing not shared. Through Jesus Christ our Lord. *Amen.*

Eternal God and loving Father, hear us as we summon into memory the stalwart men and women who begot our faith as Protestant disciples of your Son. We would be led by their light and walk in their footsteps, but save us, we pray, from imitating their eccentricities and ignoring their essence. Keep us from being no more than objectors to evil. Make us as surely promoters of good and priests in the priesthood of all believers. Justified by the faith that is in us, may we hasten the day when your kingdom will come and your will be done on the earth. Through Jesus Christ our Lord. *Amen.*

World Community Day

God of all races and peoples, Lord of every land and nation, the world is too much with us, and yet it is not. Day by day we touch it, taste it, hear it, see it, smell it; but still its magnitude escapes us, and we live as if nothing mattered that exceeded the reach of our fingers. Enlarge our vision, we pray, and grant that by our worship at this time we may be enabled to see the whole earth as our home and all of its people as our brothers and sisters. Through Jesus Christ our Lord. *Amen.*

Almighty God, who never was not and always will be, who created the world to be a home for your people and designed your people to dwell in their home without quarrel or strife, we pray for justice in all places of earth. We pray for peace. Persuade us to start building justice and peace here; lead us to begin forging them now. Through Jesus Christ our Lord. *Amen.*

O God, whose providence is confined by walls neither of time nor of space, we commend to your particular care the leaders of peoples and nations. Separate them from their pomp and circumstance, we pray, and seeing themselves as no more precious in your sight than the least of those in their governance, may they so chasten their power and curb their pride that they lift up their hearts to you, submit their decisions to your laws and your teachings, and obey your commands, made known through Jesus Christ our Lord. *Amen.*

Thanksgiving

God almighty, Lord eternal, Origin of all that is and Maker of all that is made, enable us to thank you as we ought. Forgive us when we take your creation for granted and do not thank you at all, when we thank you with no more attention than that paid the person who holds open a door before us, when we thank you with our lips but not with our lives. Quicken our senses; make us aware. Giver of all, teach us to be grateful. Through Jesus Christ our Lord. *Amen.*

Lord God almighty, we call to mind before you the stalwart folk of years long past who braved the hostile seas to build in this land a home for peace and freedom. Chasten our hearts, we pray, that being still their debtors, we may strive to pay the debt we owe them. Keep us from using our freedom to hold our sisters and brothers in bondage, and permit us no rest while any of your creatures are slaves. Empower us to be makers of peace at home and abroad, and allow us no ease while any peace is imposed by injustice. Vouchsafe that feeding on the valor of the past, we may ourselves become a new valiant past for the future. Through Jesus Christ our Lord. *Amen.*

Invisible Spirit, from whom everything came and in whom all is maintained and renewed, we thank you for our lives and for the means of their sustenance. For the air we breathe and the water we drink and the food we eat, for the sequence of the seasons and for the alternation of the night and the day, for the hills and the valleys, the seas and the rivers, for the land on which we build our homes and for the wood and stone we use to build them, for fish and birds and animals, and for all the mysteries and wonders of a universe that still eludes our full knowledge we thank you and we bless your holy name. Make us faithful stewards of your bountiful goodness, we pray. Punish any wastefulness, any careless pollution, or wanton destruction. You have entrusted us with treasure beyond our conceiving. Grant that we may not betray your trust. In Jesus' name. *Amen.*

PASTORAL PRAYERS

GENERAL PRAYERS

We Are So Small

Infinite and invisible God, beyond whom nothing is and without whom everything is not, forgive us for bothering you. We are so small, and you are so great. You have worlds to keep in order, and we have only offices and kitchens. Our swift lives disappear as a tale that is told, and you have neither end nor beginning. Pardon us then for troubling you with our own little troubles. We would leave you alone were we not so fearful of being left alone ourselves. For here and there and now and then we discover what needs no discovering at all: we cannot pull ourselves up by our own bootstraps; we cannot save ourselves.

Assembled now before you in this holy house of prayer, we acknowledge that these lives which you have given us are too intractable for us to handle long or safely. Self-made men and women, we remain unmade, and often we feel like bedclothing still unattended after the sleep of the night—dislodged from its proper anchorings, crumpled, unkempt, and awaiting the intrusion of a masterful hand. So we turn to you who first created us and pray that you will continue your creating.

Help us to outgrow our childishness, and as we mature in physical stature, foster no less our maturity in wisdom and in favor with yourself. Dissuade us from running up so many blind alleys, fleeing our fears but assuring our capture. Save us from following saviors with no power to save, from bending the knee to demagogues intent not to serve but only to use. Protect us from trusting protections not worthy of trust, building porous defenses of money and lands, of power and fame. Teach us, good Lord, that only you are the ultimate refuge and strength of your people, and keep us restless until we find our peace at last within your mighty arms. In Jesus' name. *Amen.*

Half Wanting, Half Regretting

Father eternal and almighty, from whom we came, in whom we live, and unto whom at last we go, we have gathered in this sacred place, half wanting to be where we are and half regretting our absence from the tasks that we left. Here we sit, at least in the neighborhood of other human beings and, by your grace, in the fellowship of our common devotion to yourself. We cast our minds around this room. How many universes there are beside us, before us, and behind! How many worlds peopled with the hope and the dread that we have crowded within us, the strength and the weakness, the virtue and the sin. How many souls of your own creation, begotten by your love, sustained by your power, and meant for your joy and your peace.

Often we see one another without seeing and steadily understand without understanding. Teach us, we pray, to open windows of insight amongst us, to clear roadways of encouragement, to build bridges of trust. Help us to help one another, Lord, and not to hurt. Lead us to be glad in the gladness of our brothers and sisters, and where singing is called for, let no one find us silent. Lead us to be sad in the sadness of our brothers and sisters, and where sorrow is heavy, withhold from us your comfort until we comfort those without it.

Awaken us to the need to be prepared, our Father, and prepare us to make ourselves ready. Let us not deceive ourselves about the cost of goodness, the price of peace, the dues of decency, the expense of righteousness. We pray that you will gird us daily so to live that dying daily we may daily be the means of life. Keep us different from one another, for you have fashioned in this place a body meant for many missions; but keep us one, for you have summoned your people to march toward the goal of your choosing. So may we, being apart, yet be together and, being together, find light and strength for our labors apart. Through Jesus Christ our Lord. *Amen.*

Be Patient with Us

Holy and eternal Spirit, you are patient with others more often than we wish and with us more often than we deserve. Be patient with us now as we endeavor to worship you in honesty and faithfulness. How many gods we have before yourself! How many graven images we set where none should stand but you! How many things we love without loving the One who gives them! Keep us, we pray, from thinking that we serve you while wanting you to be our servant. Save us from pretending that we speak for you when we have not even known you. Deny us peace in dealing with words but not with the Word, with facts but not with the Truth, with ways but not with the Way. Protect us from toying with theology as if it had no kinship with religion and from practicing religion as if it had no dependence on theology. Lead us not into the joy that sees not the pain of our fellows, but lead us neither into the darkness that is blind to your love. Let not our weakness leave us querulous nor our strength make us proud. Help us even when we do not want your help, and cleanse us even when we cherish our sins.

Ever coming to your creatures in the fullness of your grace, forgive us that we come to you with so little of ourselves. So much of us is still in bondage to the day we have left behind, and so much of us is leaping toward the day that lies ahead. Yet we pray that you will not disdain the will that led us to be here and that, being with us, you will so discipline our hearts and minds that we at last are nonetheless with you. Through Jesus Christ our Lord. *Amen.*

We Must Turn Your Stomach

God of our fathers and mothers, Lord of our daughters and
sons, we praise your name for what we have seen of your glory,
and we look in hope for what is yet to be. You have been great
beyond even our wonder, and when our days on earth are no
more, your wonderful greatness will stand and prevail. But
now, great Spirit of might and of mercy! *Now!* Now are the
times when we need you, here the hours when we can know
you, and these the days when we must be your servants or
never serve you at all. So briefly we live. So soon we die.

Grant then in these moments of worship a clearing of minds,
a warming of hearts, a quickening of souls. Touch us. Touch
us at the innermost depths of our beings, and transform what
you have touched. We know so much, so much and so little—
too much to be excused for our wickedness, too little to be safe
in our wisdom. Our love is so strong, so strong and so fragile—
strong enough to be kind to the kindly, frail enough to be
shattered on the neighbor next door. We are so keenly alive, so
keenly alive and so dead—alive enough to hurt when others
assail us, dead enough to feel no pain when others hurt. Grant
us then in these moments of worship a clearing of minds, a
warming of hearts, a quickening of souls.

Save us from praising prayer but never praying, expecting
gifts but not giving, preaching belief but not believing, damn-
ing sin but glibly sinning. We are often so pious, our Father, so
sweetly and softly and whipped-creamedly righteous while all
around us the harsh and hungry world exists as if for us it had
no existence. We must turn your stomach. Yet we are often so
cultured, our Father, so proudly and snobbishly and upturned-
nosedly sophisticated while the created disown their Creator
and souls begotten pretend to be their own begetters. We must
make you laugh.

O shake us up, and shake us down, that being down we may
be lifted up by you in peace and light, in strength and faith, in
truth and hope and love forevermore. Through Jesus Christ our
Lord. *Amen.*

While the Dew of the Morning

Eternal Spirit, come to us while the dew of the morning is still on the grass, abide with us through the heat of the day, and calm us to sleep when the twilight has fallen. Be here among us now, while the morning moves onward to noon and part of the day is behind us and part of it yet to be lived. Let this hour spent together be a mountain peak of vision, Lord. We know not how our deepest insights come nor understand the way in which we sometimes have the sense of seeing you as face to face, but we ask that, here among our peers bowing with us in our common need of you, our hearts may be touched by your power and saved for your purpose.

From the fears that so easily beset us, from the fretfulness of petty irritations and the weariness of unimportant failures, from the nagging of envy and the sleeplessness of what we want but cannot have—emancipate our spirits, our Father. Lead us until we set our feet on upward trails and fix our eyes on far horizons. Be to us a wind from lofty heights driving out the stagnant vapors of our fearfulness and fright. As cleansing waters, bathe our souls, purging them of sin and wrong. And out of all the multitude of hungers that assail us, bind our souls to one embracing duty that shall keep us close to you.

You know this church as none but you can know. Be then a blessing in each home within our fellowship: the homes where there is illness or pain of any kind, the broken homes where love has long since gone and where only bitterness remains, the empty homes with vacant spaces where the loved ones used to be, the anxious homes where problems writhe unsolved and angry choices battle for decisions. Open our hearts that we may be aware of those who stand in need of us within our very midst. Guide us to love one another and to bear one another's burdens in the blessed comradeship of those who own a common Lord. We are a chosen people. Set us then apart and make us different. Cause us to dwell so close to you that others take notice of us that we have been with him of whom we speak. Through Jesus Christ our Lord. *Amen.*

You Can Do All Things

You can do all things, our Father. Whatsoever lies within the realm of possibility lies also in your power to perform and bring to pass. You are might beyond our thinking, and you are goodness altogether. What you will for your human creatures is the largest life for each of them; and all your ways are righteousness, and all your paths are peace.

But *we* cannot do all things, Lord, and we are unsure whether the things we do are right or wise or good. We are so blind. We are so deaf. We are so lacking in perception of the things we ought to understand; and when we think about our inner selves, it is as if we thought of strangers. When we turn to other men and women, we see them not as sons and daughters of our common Father, but as competitors for some prize or place we want ourselves. When we lift our minds toward you, the burden often seems so heavy that we drop it quickly to the earth again and never really comprehend at all the things you ask of us.

So we pray that you will clean our minds, our Father—wash their windows, air their unsunned spaces, dust their dark and musty corners, scrub their walls and floors until they shine as once they did when first you made them long ago. Unbend the hearts long twisted by jealousy of those of whom we have no cause to be jealous, by hatred of those we ought to love, by fear of things that have no power to hurt us, and by dread of duties meant to be blessings. Raise up the souls bowed down by guilt for sins that you have long since forgiven, by weakness that—if we would use it—you could shape to magnify your power, by sorrows which—if we would loose them—you could even make a source of strength to us. Keep us from being foolish in the sense that we never use the brains you gave us, but keep us from being foolish also in the sense that we ascribe omniscience to those brains.

You have revealed yourself to us in Jesus Christ. Persuade us to trust that revelation, draw our sustenance from it; to seek our courage in it, plot our journey by it; to build our faith upon it, live in hope because of it. In Jesus' name. *Amen.*

For Corporations and Other Businesses

God of all worlds and lands, Lord of every nation and people, before we forget you, we pause to remember. It is you who are the Creator and we the created—you who are mighty and we who are weak, you who are deathless and we who are mortal, you who see and we who are blind. Grant us wider horizons than our daily duties, nobler ends than our selfish advantage, brighter hopes than our peace and contentment, stronger foundations than our budgets and balances.

We know that skies might be clean, our Father, and earth could be fair. Life might have glory and humankind grandeur. Help us not to handle carelessly these gifts of yours not lightly given. It is a tale of souls that our computers tell, each word a mind that thinks and plans and struggles, each number a heart that fears and hurts and dreams. Aid us so to hold the fragile tenderness of life that we may not wound more deeply souls already deeply wounded.

We pray that all corporations and other businesses may be bodies fitly joined in all their parts, strong to meet the needs that offer honest warrant for their being—humble enough to be righteous, wise enough to be gentle, patient enough to be kind. For ourselves as officers, workers, or holders of stock in these institutions, we pray that we may not be content until we are whole persons in your sight. To work, to play, to love, to worship—to all of them we would give ourselves, but to each in proper room and proportion. Prod us to understand that if we are not bigger than our jobs, we are too small for them. Bestow upon us sufficient faith in your providence to let the universe sometimes proceed without our guidance. Enlarge our affections until they include every corner of the earth, but never let us forget to care for the loved ones nearest to home. Lead us to reverence the altars that bespeak our human dependence, but guard us lest we choose the wrong gods for our praise. And yours be the kingdom and the power and the glory forever. *Amen.*

You Are Quiet and Still

God of might, Father of mercy, always beyond us yet ever within, we long to speak to you and know that you have truly heard. But what if long since you already have heard and overheard? We are not proud of all that we have said in other days, not happy even about all that we have prayed. Better, Lord, that you should speak to us and that we should truly hear. But you are quiet and still. What do you mean by your silences, Lord? What do you intend when you act and not explain, give and not interpret, withhold and not show cause?

Could it be that you have already spoken and still daily speak? Is there silence because you have not spoken or because we stopped our ears against your speaking? Do we seek, or fearing to find, seek only failure in our seeking? Has the Second Coming of your Son been so long delayed because his first has been so long rejected? What more could he say than already he has said, and how could you speak more clearly than daily you speak through his life and his words?

Disciples of your Son, we want reward for our discipleship, but already we have it. Save us from having had it. Through Jesus Christ our Lord. *Amen.*

From Thoughts in Ignorance

Almighty God, Father of our Lord Jesus Christ, Holy Spirit ever near your people, we turn toward you, we face you, we wait upon you. From thoughts conceived in ignorance, from words born of anger, from deeds done to hurt, and from lives lived in selfishness, we come to this place built to your glory. Noisy, we ought to have been quiet; frantic, we ought to have been still; fearful, we ought to have been confident; and hateful, we ought to have been kind. We are not worthy to be called your children, but you are yet our Father; and what you created you can cleanse and save. So we turn toward you, we face you, we wait upon you; and we pray that you will not cast us from your presence nor leave us helpless where we have no help but you.

Let your Spirit rest in special power on this congregation, Lord. Through so many yesterdays we have met in this place; through so many yesterdays we have shared the work and worship of these rooms; through so many yesterdays we have borne each other's burdens in the common quest for strength to do your will. Today we hunger for you once again, and as we face the week before us, we know that we shall walk alone if you are not beside us. So be with us now, and go with us then; and in our joys and in our sorrows, in our defeats and in our victories, be our truth, our way, our life.

Save us from the fear that theologians have reduced you to a symbol or that scientists have transformed you to a process. Fix fast our faith in your Son, and grant that owning him as our Lord, we may not be too proud to cede our Lord our faithfulness. Give us steadiness in what our fathers and mothers believed; and in our thought of days to come, grant that we may find the means of hope but not of escape.

Surround us with yourself, our Father. Permit us no flight from your presence. Accept no substitutes for loyalty. Tolerate no compromises with obedience. Be content with no carelessness, lenient with no evasions, blind to no pretensions. In the ruthlessness of love build firm the lives here offered for your service, and so invade our souls that in the awesome actuality of now we become new bodies for your mighty and merciful Spirit. In Jesus' name. *Amen.*

If There Be Those Among Us

God of ages past, Lord of present years, and Oversoul of all the time to be, you guided our fathers and mothers in their pilgrimage and wait no less to guide their children. To you we turn as thirsty people to a fountain flowing. Ever have you been our haven and stronghold, and even in the hours when we knew it not, still were you the sanctuary never failing. So to you we bring this day all that we are and ever dream to be, confessing that apart from your power there is nothing that can shelter or save.

If there be those among us who face separation from loved ones, with months or years of not seeing or touching, let each find a lodgment of heart in yourself, and though the days be many and the miles be long, bind each to the other in their bondage to you—apart but together, still one though two. If there be those among us who carry the burden of some great pain and live always so crushed by its load that strength disappears and hope is lost, lift up their eyes to the hills whence all our help descends, and teach them how wonderful is your might when all else falters and fails. If there be those among us who have done what is evil in your sight and never face dawn without the dread of their guilt, reveal to them how great is your mercy to them who do truly and earnestly repent of their sins. If there be those among us blessed with abundance in body and soul yet still striving steadfastly for none but themselves, lead them back to the light, and replenish their strength as they give it away.

Lord, as best we can, we call to mind all of your people in all of the world. So instruct us, we pray, in the ministries of your love that we become the bearers of your healing peace to some who suffer pain or hardship. Empower your true servants everywhere that they do your will in faithful courage, and to you be the kingdom and the power and the glory forever. *Amen.*

We Know So Little

God almighty, eternal in the heavens and ever more than we can surely see or fully know, we bow before you, still our minds before you, open our hearts before you. We know so little, Lord, and there is so great a realm of darkness around the tiny circle of our light. We walk as those whose eyes had never been unsealed and whose ears never unstopped; and as weeks pass into years, we take our ignorance of you for granted, assuming that as we live today, so shall we always live.

O shatter this stoic resignation, Lord. Break through the walls of selfishness and fear by which we keep you from ourselves. Assure us that your will is love, that you call the least of us by name, and that you covet for us only what is best for us. Save us from the insecurity that ever must disguise its frailty as might, lest, seeing us as in the truest sense that we are, our peers laugh at us and speak of us with pity or with scorn. Convince us that the smallest of us is as precious in your sight as the greatest, that you hold for us a place that no one else can fill, and that no circumstance of death or life can dislodge a single child of yours from sight or care or power to befriend.

Persuade us that we seek your will through faithful reading of the holy Scriptures, and keep us steady in that reading even when it seems no more than drudgery. Guide us into habits of prayer and meditation, and hold us to those habits through the hours when they seem to bear no fruit but weariness. Keep us from thinking that we can be good alone, and so command our straying wills that Sunday by Sunday we are found in worship with our sisters and our brothers. And when the quiet time is past, grant us to be as much the body of your Son throughout the week as we have been on Sunday: his mind to think your thoughts after you, his hands to do your deeds of love and mercy, his feet to run your errands of goodwill, his lips to speak your words of healing and of helpfulness. For we dedicate ourselves afresh to you and pledge that as you give us strength and wisdom, we shall do as you would have us do. Through Jesus Christ our Lord. *Amen.*

We Still Our Hearts

Eternal Father, Holy Spirit, we come to you in the quiet of a Sunday morning, and we still our hearts and pray that you will speak and we may hear. From many different ways we come— from office and store, from campus and hospital, from the open road and the kitchen stove and the lonely room. In many different minds we come—the ones who find in you a friend as real as anyone they know on earth, the ones who think of you as nothing but a puppet for their fantasizing, the ones who desiccate you into beauty, truth, or goodness. In many different needs we come—in strength and the need that you command us, in weakness and the need that you renew us, in sorrow and the need that you console us. As each has want of you, be known to each, we pray, and grant that each may leave this place with faith rebuilt and hope restored.

We pray for those who bear upon themselves the burden of loss or bewilderment. Send our minds and hearts to dwell with them, and spur our hands and feet to do for them what you would have us do. We pray for those about to face some sorrow unforeseen, some bereavement unexpected, some temptation unannounced. Walk with them through the valley of the shadow, and vouchsafe that with them, too, may be the ones among us here who can best add comfort to their journey. We pray for the young, that they may not grow old in bitterness; for those of middle years, that they may do good deeds with diligence; for the aged, that in sunset time they may have peace.

Broaden our vision, Lord. Deny us the sin of looking only at ourselves. We are your creatures: cause us then to act as if we were. We are your children: shape us then until we bear upon our hearts the marks of the One we call our Father. Through Jesus Christ our Lord. *Amen.*

In Retirement

God of light and of shadow, revealed but still hidden, your will is past our finding out, your ways beyond our knowing. Whence we came we understand only in part, and why we are here and whither we go are mysteries exceeding all our comprehension. Soon or late we recognize that we are mortal, and as our time of life on earth winds down in prospect, we pray that you will give us wisdom for the journey before us.

Save us from holding on too long or letting go too soon, and when the hour strikes for us to shut the store or close the desk or put away the tools, deny us self-pity, shield us from resentment, protect us from fear. Spare us the sins of arrogance, but withhold not from us the happiness of honest pride. Grant us satisfaction in miles traveled and plateaus reached, words spoken and chapters written, meals cooked and children reared, houses built and planes flown, minds calmed and bodies healed, strength bestowed and love shared. When we have done what we can, let there be no guilt that we do not what we can't.

Nevertheless, our Father, we would not so identify what we are with what we have done that, ending our formal employment, we assume that we have put an end to our reason for being. Were we not before ever we held a job, and did not life seem then experience to be cherished? All through the days when we worked for our living was not life much more than our working, and was not meaning as frequently found apart from our labor as in it? Break now, we pray, our lifelong bonding of doing work and being paid. Instruct us in the blessedness of giving with no wish for return. Lure us into kindnesses that pledge no compensation. Volunteer us for armies that fight only injustice. Prompt our hands to build homes for the homeless, cook food for the hungry. Warm our hearts to call on the sick and comfort the lonely, love the unlovely and bring hope to the hopeless. Living, we live by your choosing; else clearly we should not be living. Teach us not to waste the precious gifts you still bestow upon us. Retired, we are no less surely disciples of your Son. Keep us faithful in his service. *Amen.*

Make Us Whole

God of might and Lord of love, greater than we can imagine and wiser than we can comprehend, patient with us beyond our deserving and generous past anything we can ask or desire, again we assemble in worship, and once more we lift our hearts to you and pray that you will make us whole. The sights of earth are ever in our eyes, O Lord, and fascinated by their glory, we find it hard to doubt their significance. The sounds of earth are ever in our ears, O Lord, and deafened by their din, we struggle in vain to hear the quiet voice that speaks of sound and fury meaning nothing. We are imperfect, unfinished, incomplete; and we pray that you will continue in us the creation begun at our birth. We pray that you will make us whole.

We are often brakes when we ought to be pistons, our Father, frequently dams when we ought to be channels. We are steadily frightened when we ought to be fearless, cruel when we ought to be kind, stingy when we ought to be bountiful. Proud of our freedom, we are the prisoners of our own insecurities, and claiming not to be the slaves of anyone, we daily do obeisance to our guilt and our jealousy, our lust and our greed.

Strike the chains of meanness from our souls, we beseech you. Chop away the bonds of doubt and fear. Drive us out of the caves of dread and despair; and in the wide and sunny spaces of your love, renew in us the faith that does not die. We are your creatures, your children. We are your comrades in your toil and travail on the earth. So we would wake from our sleep, rise from our beds, lift up our hearts, pledge our lives. No longer would we be imperfect, unfinished, incomplete. We would be whole, and wholly yours. Through Jesus Christ our Lord. *Amen.*

In Troubled Times

We turn to you in troubled times, our Father. Daily in the newspapers we read of hatred and violence, war and crime, greed and lust and mental disturbance. We know that humankind was made for better life than this, and wanting to change the world, we find ourselves frustrated at every turn. Being frustrated, we grow anxious; and grown anxious, we become restive and fretful and bitter. So much is wrong with the world, our Father. So much is wrong with ourselves. We want to help, but we know not how. So we turn to you as little children, asking you to help us in our helplessness.

Grant that we may hold fast our sense of perspective, for though we are living in tumultuous days, we need to remember the centuries of tumult that preceded our generation and that doubtless will follow it. Keep us from being so upset about everything that we fasten on anything as the scapegoat; and save us from accusations having no other ground than our weakness and from resentments with no other source than our envy. Grant us that in any time of disagreement we speak as in your presence, and calm us until in strife we seek not so much to conquer the one with whom we stand at odds as to let your will control the struggle and give you charge of what we say and do.

We live among a multitude of fearful people, Lord, and we are often fearful, too: afraid of high prices and still higher prices, afraid of high taxes and still higher taxes, afraid of accidents and war, afraid of disease and old age and insecurity. Encourage us, we pray, to believe what we say we believe, to put in you the trust not only of words but also of bodies and souls and to find in your Son not simply someone nice enough for children to become acquainted with but also him who judges all we are and all we do. If we know we need you, we beg you to fill the need we know; and if we do not know we need you, we urge you to disconcert us until we do. Through Jesus Christ our Lord. *Amen.*

In Your Own Image

Almighty God, Eternal Father, who created us in your own image and fashioned us in honor and glory until we stood but little lower than the angels in your sight, we ask your help in managing the life that you have given us.

So much there is of wonder and beauty in it, Lord; so great the reason for faith and confidence and joy. Yet we often stand in the shadows, living many days in darkness, dwelling frequently like those condemned to torture, misery, or death. Stir us to lift up our eyes to the hills and far beyond them to you, from whom comes strength for any need we have or evermore shall have. Teach us why we need not be afraid, why jealousy is suicide and hatred self-defeating. As members of your church, we belong to the family of those who seek to serve you. Lead us then to live indeed as members of that family, and to it give full measure of our capabilities, and from it humbly take the aid it has to offer us.

Save us from the arrogance that makes us think that we can stand alone and from the selfishness that is content to receive but not to share. When we lose our jobs, send deep our roots to soil no circumstance of life can alter. When friends prove false, keep sweet the springs that feed our souls, lest bitterness in them make all our living bitter, too. In sorrow save us from despair and in victory from pompousness. Keep us from smiling on the mighty and despising them of low degree. Defend us from counting anyone beyond redemption. Protect us from being patient with customers, friends, and even enemies, while loosing vengefulness on husbands or wives or children in our homes.

Assist us to learn what things are good and what things bad, what things great and what things small, what things wise and what things foolish; and grant us then the wisdom not to sell eternity for time, neither barter the priceless for trash beneath price. We pray that we may have the courage of the faith we profess, the bravery to bet our lives that you are truly God our Father, the fortitude to own the Christ as Lord and follow him wherever he may go. Hear our prayer, we beseech you, and open our hearts to your answer. In Jesus' name. *Amen.*

We Dedicate Our Homes

From our homes we have come to this church today, our Father, and back to our homes we soon shall go. This is the house we have built to your praise and your glory. Here we feel most surely your presence among us, and we would not handle carelessly the signs and symbols of your power and your grace. Yet were not, too, our homes intended to be holy, and are not you as often there as here? Did you not create your people to dwell together in families, and do you never yearn for comradeship in humble places?

Grant then, Lord, your blessing on the homes here represented. To you we dedicate their strength and aspirations, and we pray that each may be to you sure means whereby your will takes root and prospers.

Strengthen their walls that they may hold stoutly within them whatsoever things are true and honorable, whatsoever things are just and pure, whatsoever things are lovely and gracious. *Strengthen their walls* that they may shelter behind them love and joy and peace, patience and kindness and goodness, faithfulness and gentleness and self-control. *Strengthen their walls* that they may keep sternly out the works of enmity and strife, jealousy and anger, selfishness and dissension.

We pray for mothers and fathers that they may be tender and strong; we pray for children that in the sturdy gentleness of their parents they may find guidance enough to save them from falling and freedom sufficient to nourish their growing. Let our homes be places of refuge, Lord: bulwarks of rest and trust and peace; but let them, too, be points of departure: gateways to a world that calls for our help. Lead us to speak the love we often hold in silence. Teach us the grace of gratitude. Guard us against pouting, sulking, nagging, and holding grudges. Show us how to accept and be accepted, to forgive and be forgiven; and grant us the courage to open our hearts to you that in your holy presence our homes, too, may be holy. Through Jesus Christ our Lord. *Amen.*

We Hear in Part

God of all ages, Lord of all worlds, Father, Son, and Holy Spirit, you call us to be disciples in your service, and wait, and call and wait, and wait and call again. We hear in part, and in even lesser part we heed. You truly live and move and have a being, Lord— or do you not? You are indeed our bulwark and our strength and in trouble such a present help that the mountains may shake and we not fear—or are you not? One day we believe, but the next we do not believe at all. Each of us one, we are yet many, and in the inner recesses so much of us is at war with the rest of us that often there is no peace for any of us. No peace and little power; for half of us heading east and the other half west, we never move beyond the act of heading. We call ourselves Christians, but we are often stalled Christians, for even unobstructed, many times we coast and coast and ever slower coast until one day we discover that we have wholly ceased to move.

Yet, Lord, we do not want to stop; we want to march. We want to dare and do, and if it be your will, to die the death that conquers dying. Disciples in name, we want to be disciples in deed. We want to serve and through our service multiply your servants. So we come to you in hope that you will do for us what we have tried to do for ourselves, and done perhaps in part, but in much larger part have simply left undone.

Clean us out, our Father. Our souls are blocked, clogged, stuffed with fear and doubt, with lust and greed, with envy, pride, and hatred. Clean us out, our Father, and then fill us up. Truth and honesty, courage and patience, tenderness and compassion, joy and thanksgiving—how we hunger for them, Lord, but how we tremble at the thought that they might one day take command of us. How we thirst after them, Lord, but only when we have a hand upon the spigot and can turn them off at will. Do with us then what we wish you had already done with us but dread to have you do. It would be happiness untold to have lost our lives and found them; lead us at least to be willing to lose them. Flood us with the love of goodness. Make us better than we want to be, braver than we dare to be, kinder than we have the heart to be, stronger than we have the strength to be; and to you be all the glory and to you all the praise. Through Jesus Christ our Lord. *Amen.*

Silently Now

Silently now we wait upon God, and then in quietness and confidence we lift from hearts that love him words that seek his presence, and his power, his will, and his peace.

Let us thank God for the bright things that still shine through the darkness: for the steadiness with which the seasons advance and the days proceed, for the men and women who have not lost faith in the healing ways of love and mercy, for the beauty of landscape and friendship, of music and laughter, of sculpture and sports, of travel and painting.

Let us thank God for the heartening memories of the days that are gone; for the great names of the faith that we claim: for Amos and Isaiah and Jeremiah, for Jesus and Peter and Paul, for Saint Augustine and Saint Francis and Luther, and for all the other valiant souls, especially women, nameless to those who look for names in history, but named indeed by the One who made them and by those to whom they still remain a blessed heritage.

Let us pray for men and women of every race and nation, every class and creed: the rich and the poor, the wise and the foolish, the healthy and the ill, parents who have lost their children and children their parents, the young and the old, people in prisons and refugee camps, the unemployed, the bewildered, the lonely.

Let us pray for ourselves: that our faith may be undimmed by the storms that rage so frequently around us, that our feet may be planted on rock unmoved and unmovable, that privilege may be in us a reason not for arrogance but for stewardship, and that God may keep us impervious to assaults of irritation and hatred, of bitterness and lust and hardness of heart.

Let us pray for the mission of Christ in the world: that God's kingdom may come and God's will be done in part through common human beings like ourselves and that leaving to God the tasks we cannot perform, we accept the ones that we can.

Grant, Lord, that the words now spoken and the prayers here offered may be compliant with your mighty undertakings: instruments of your will, tools of your grace. Through Jesus Christ our Lord. *Amen.*

Apart Through Summer Months

From many a severed way we come again to meet within these hallowed walls, our Father: from ocean and river, from mountain and vale, from office and kitchen and school. Apart through summer months, we yet have known that we were one in you and in the comradeship we share by membership in this our chosen church. So we celebrate today a fact long known and cherished, and from many tongues and hearts we lift to you the praise of those who seek again to serve your kingdom on this church's avenues of fellowship and labor.

Grant now that minds with many cares and problems may increasingly be taught to choose aright between the good and the bad, the wise and the silly, the large and the small. Vouchsafe that souls beset by many doubts and fears may quickly find in you the light that is not quenched, the rock that is not moved. Keep us from such hunger to be perfect that we overlook the need to be good. Save us from so many plans for tomorrow that we never live in strength and joy today. Preserve us from declaring that we would gladly die for you, but refusing to live for you when you hold before us opportunities no more distant than our fingertips.

Open our eyes to the loneliness filling the hearts of those we meet along the crowded ways: the wistful aspirations, the unfulfilled dreams, the shyness masquerading as arrogance, the jealousies and the hatred of those jealousies, the lusts and the loathing of those lusts, the struggle toward a God-intended selfhood and the failure in the struggling. As we would be forgiven, help us to forgive; and rejoicing in the wonderful diversity of your creation, may we, your children, link souls and arms with all of our brothers and sisters in the one vast family of earth owning you as its Father. Teach us to turn from inward things to outward, and with power gained in prayer and worship give might to truth and justice day by passing day. For again we say we love you, and again we pledge ourselves to be disciples of your Son, in whose name we pray. *Amen.*

Come Now in Strength

Father Almighty, Maker of heaven and earth and Giver of every good and perfect gift, in love we open our hearts to you and offer thanks for the brightness that you have shed so steadily upon our earthly way.

For the world in which we live, for the glory of field and woodland, for the fruitfulness of garden and orchard and vine, we give you grateful praise and pray that you will teach us so to hold your earth in holy trust that none may be hungry, neither cold nor in want of any kind. For the knowledge of your Son, for the powerful beauty of his life on the earth, for the word he brings of you, and for the good news that underneath all our frailty and fearfulness are the everlasting arms of your care, we give you grateful praise, and pray that no might of the world may rend us from your will or tear us from your way. For husband or wife, for brother or sister, for parent or child we give you grateful praise, and pray that you will guard the people of our homes when danger comes, or fear, or any trial of their faith and hope.

Come now in strength, O God, to those who bear in heavy pain the burden of things that might have been. Come now in healing and peace.

You know how long is the path when our souls are laden with the deeds that we have wrongly done, how sharp the anguish when our hearts feel the shame of the good that we did not do, how bitter the remorse when we taste at last the vanity of life spent for no one but ourselves. From the condemnation of things that cannot be changed, from all that makes our past a world of recollections unhappy and hateful, from words wrongly spoken and deeds badly done, from hurt given in anger and harm wrought in blindness or in full knowledge of the evil being done, save us, our Father. For you can save, and you alone. The years are yours, and the ruling thereof: the moments wherein we live today but the yesterdays, too, and the tomorrows as well. So being your children, we hasten to you like the son of old who returned to his father. Restore us, we pray, to yourself, and in the end we shall not fear though death should come, or life. Through Jesus Christ our Lord. *Amen.*

From Differing Ways

Almighty God, eternal Father, from differing ways we come to this place and in manifold thoughts and hopes and fears, but together in this sacred hour we join our hearts as one and ask that you hear and help us as we pray.

As each has need of strength beyond that now possessed, let each entreat God's presence: the fearful, that God may still the fear; the weak, that God may empower the frailty; the strong, that God may command the might; the sinful, that God may stir repentance; the lonely, that God may bring comfort. In silence now, as each has need of strength beyond that now possessed, let each of us entreat God's presence in our minds and hearts.

Let each of us remember ones held dear and ask God's blessing on their lives today: someone who lies at home infirm or ill, someone in a nursing home or hospital, someone who has newly lost a person deeply loved, someone facing choices and alone not able to make them. Let each of us name silently to God the ones we love who need God's special grace.

Let each of us commend to God's discipline those who hold the fate of nations in their keeping: presidents and dictators and kings and queens. Let us remember the delegates to the United Nations, the legislators in our own and other countries' council chambers, the men and women everywhere who shape their peoples' policies with other peoples. Let each of us pray earnestly that God may capture their submission and obedience, lure them to justice, and guide them to peace.

Let us summon to mind this church of which we are ourselves a portion. Let us think about all it has been in the days that are gone, all it is now, and all it yet can be. Let us pray for ourselves that as we assume its privileges, we also take up its burdens and that the service we render may be that of hands and feet no less than lips and tongues.

Lord, you have heard the prayers that have been spoken in these moments and heard, too, the petitions unspoken in our hearts. Answer, we beseech you, as may be most expedient in your sight. Through Jesus Christ our Lord. *Amen.*

Blessing Church Leaders

Spirit of all power and grace, from whose Son, Jesus Christ, comes our summons to serve your holy purposes for earth, we set apart for your blessing these leaders of this church and congregation. Chosen for their tasks by those who found them worthy, they have accepted the burdens proposed for their shoulders, and now we seek your confirmation and empowerment.

People of the laity, they are none the less ministers of this ministering community, priests in the priesthood of all believers, disciples in the honored band that once included Peter and James and John. Grant then that they may not handle carelessly the sacred things entrusted to their keeping. Called to point the way before us in their leadership, they will want to walk the second mile in all they do among us, but suffer them not to scorn the first. Outside these walls and within, steel them to be truthful in what they say and honest in what they do. Let them be punctual in meeting accepted appointments, dependable in fulfilling appropriate responsibilities, staunch in supporting their comrades in office. Teach them to control both their pride and their tempers and to be calm in controversy, patient in misunderstanding, and tolerant of ignorance. We want our leaders to be distinctively Christian, our Father, but first of all we seek in them the wholesomeness of good men and women.

Yet, of course, we hunger and thirst for more, and as we set apart our leaders for your blessing, we wonder. Is there someone here who has read again the holy documents of faith and found among them the very truth about yourself and your Son, who has thought again about the church and yearned to make it in fact more fully the body of Christ, who has recalled again the vows taken at baptism and now at last in this place and at this time makes an offering of life in commitment to service? If such be among us, we pray that through the mouths of this leadership here consecrated you will blow the spark to flame and kindle a fire of new hope for your people. So move, too, we ask, in the hearts of all who offer themselves as officers of this congregation. Thrust them into kindnesses for which they think they are not able. Tempt them into braveries that cause their knees to tremble. Nudge them into commitments that now would seem impossible, and henceforth let this day stand in memory as one when long steps were taken and great bridges were crossed. Through Jesus Christ our Lord. *Amen.*

Never Absent, Never Tardy

Eternal God, never absent, never tardy, whose rule is on far lands beyond our knowing, you reign as well where humankind can learn your purposes if once we set our hearts upon their quest. We assemble again in this house erected to your praise, and we ask that you enable us to do the deed for which we come.

Help us to worship you, O Lord. Save us from wandering thoughts and chaotic affections, and capture our minds with your majesty and glory, your purity and holiness, your goodness and love. Help us to wait for you, O Lord. Keep us from such engrossment with our petty obsessions that we have no time for your mighty commands, and guard us against so filling ourselves with dread and anxiety that we have no room for trust and assurance. Help us to answer you, O Lord. Prevent us from finding peace before we should, from hearing your Word but never asking what it means for ourselves, from being no better human beings at the end of our worship than we were at its start. Grant that through each coming day we may respond to your call by sound words spoken and brave deeds done.

Father of truth and goodness, who drew near your people of old and quickened in them such thought of yourself that no other thought could invade or prevail, speak to us, we pray, and so permeate our souls that we own no Lord but yourself. We look with apprehension on the earthly objects clamoring to seize our uttermost allegiance, and we call on you to aid us in our struggle. Grant that we may fasten our eyes upon you, call you God and you alone, pledge you our loyalty and none but you. Encourage us to love our country and serve its worthy purposes with faithfulness, but should a conflict rise between the nation's insistence and yours, let us not tremble to stand at your side. Incite us to be diligent in the tasks by which we earn our daily bread, but should they seek in us a work against your purpose, enable us to give them no hearing. So may we be agents of your holy will and find fellowship with all who love and serve you. Through Jesus Christ our Lord. *Amen.*

The Leaders of Earth's Nations and Peoples

Almighty and eternal God, you who have needs that only human hearts and hands can satisfy and whose power is often revealed through human action, we call to your remembrance the leaders of earth's nations and peoples. No one knows better than you how fearfully the peace and justice of the world depend on those leaders, and we pray that they may not betray their stewardship, neither mistake the nature of their obligations.

When they think of themselves, let them never doubt that those not with you are against you, and may they not deal lightly with their own weaknesses and sins. Save them from craving adulation as gods when they have not even earned respect as decent human beings. Grant them never to be so anxious about the specks in other people's eyes that they do not see the logs in their own. Guide them not to feed upon their people but to feed them, and not to think that praising justice excuses them from doing it. Chasten them to honesty and kindness, and deny them the complacency that they are too important to obey their own laws. By whatever name they call you, vouchsafe that they stand with you, work for you, and bear with you the heavy yokes of righteousness and truth.

Yet we pray, too, that when these leaders of their nations and their peoples think of others than themselves, they may hear the kindred word that those not against you are for you. Let the iron of your justice disincline them to the softness that is stranger to fact, but drain not their veins of the blood of compassion. Impel them to use with full passion the talents you gave them, but foster alive in their hearts the awareness that you have many witnesses and many loves and many mysteries. They see only in part, O Lord, as do all of your children, but we ask that you push afar their horizons: that you so lengthen their sight and enlarge their sympathies that they find no man so ugly or woman so troublesome or child so insignificant that they close the door against need or shut their eyes upon hope. Through Jesus Christ our Lord. *Amen.*

Wrestled to Quietness

God of truth and grace, Holy Spirit ever near us when we pray, we wrestle ourselves to quietness; we fasten ourselves to stillness; and we force our minds to think of you and to seek the meaning of our lives in this world that you have made. We have pledged ourselves to be disciples of your Son, and you know with what blendings of strength and of weakness we have made that commitment, with what fusions of wisdom and folly, with what alternations of hope and despair for your church and your people beyond it.

Unabashedly we pray for ourselves. We ask for vision, that we may learn to separate fact from fantasy, truth from falsehood, right from wrong; and clearly comprehending fact and truth and right, may we firmly love what we have comprehended. We ask for restlessness, that the agonies of our sisters and brothers may not be distant from our hearts, that time may prove too precious to be wasted, and that we may quickly probe the cries of hurt until we find in them the call that justifies our calling. We ask for love, that our compassion may be as your own and that liking the likable, we may not compound the world's hatred by hating the hateful. And we ask for hunger of soul, that the horizons of earth may not be sufficient horizons, that the comforts of sense may cease to be adequate comforts, that preoccupation with good causes may not leave us blind to the cause of their goodness, and that wanting to be worthy disciples of your Son, we may pay without exception the cost of that discipleship.

Especially now do we pray for our lives spent together as Christians in this church. It is not easy so to live, and wickedness is never more loathsome than grinning through the mask of righteousness and piety. We shall understand and misunderstand each other. We shall like and dislike. We shall please and annoy. We shall be right and thought wrong, and we shall be wrong while sure that we are right. Be in truth and grace among us, our Father, and grant that in this place we may fashion with your help those virtues in ourselves that we covet for the world. We are your children: you have made us, and of your deeds that deed is done. But do for us a further deed, we pray: teach us so to live together here that we give you no cause to regret your begetting. Through Jesus Christ our Lord. *Amen.*

Not to Rest Ourselves

Almighty God and merciful Father, we have met not to rest ourselves but to worship you, and we pray that you will save us from trying to create you in our own image. Keep us from striving to reduce you to our own terms, to compress you within our own horizons, to stain you with our own sins. Repudiate the bits that we struggle to place in your mouth and the reins whereby we strain to turn you in our own directions. Remain unmanageable. Stay incomprehensible. Renew again the ancient law that they remove their shoes who stand before the holy fire. We acknowledge our need of your mercy, but do not be so tender with us that we grow too flabby to fight in your wars.

Admit us, we pray, to your work in creation. Not in the sense that we stand in a void, snap our fingers, and behold a new thing we have made. Rather, grant us so to respond to the world of your shaping, so to interpret its meaning, and so employ its resources that we offer you in our bodies and minds new creatures, fit bearers of your designated burdens and trustworthy stewards of your purposeful grace. Deny us the comfort of being passengers when we ought to be members of the crew, being spectators when we ought to be members of the team, or being an audience when we ought to be members of the orchestra. Spare us the guilt of wanting always to be cosseted and cuddled, flattered and cajoled, amused and entertained. Let not the forming of a world and its people appear to us a facile act, nor one exempt from agony and anguish, nor one completed already or likely to be ended in ages foreseen or ever foreseeable. Throw us then into the fray as those on whom in large part the issue depends. Induce us to be pullers and thrusters, climbers and diggers, lifters and porters, builders and movers. Beget in us a hunger for labor beside you, a thirst for toil at your bidding. Through Jesus Christ our Lord. *Amen.*

We Need You

Everlasting God, you who existed before any other existence and are still to remain though all else wither and fail, we need you. More even than we know, we need you, and we pray that you will not lead us into temptation that we can neither recognize nor overcome and that you will deliver us from evil that beckons in the guise of the good. You have called us to be disciples of your Son; breed in us the confidence of them who know the origin of what they say, but save us from the arrogance of those who speak as if your kingdom were their own. You have summoned us to be priests in the priesthood of all believers; teach us to be mediators of your grace to those who else would never know you, but prevent us from living as if we owned that grace ourselves.

The road is narrow, Lord, that leads between your people and your throne, and if we have sat down squarely in some other person's way, take us by the hand and pull us from it. Keep us from getting in the path of your purpose.

Preserve us from growing uneasy that we are not you. Shove us out of the places set aside for yourself, and as soon as we have played our little parts upon the stage of your designing, catch us up that they who watch may think of us no more, lest perchance we steal the scene from you who can alone make lordly use of it.

As best we can, we approach you now without pretension, our Father. Once again we commit ourselves to your leading, and we pray that you will accept and confirm the commitment. Cut out of us the frailty that makes us dread the thought of ever being found in error. Plough up from us the fear that leaves us so often positive, and wrong. Burn away from us the selfishness that draws us from your will. In our heart of hearts we love you, and in our soul of souls we want to be faithful disciples of your Son, Jesus Christ, in whose name and for whose sake we offer you this prayer. *Amen.*

We Know Our Need of You

We have come to church today, our Father, because we know our need of you. We thought that we could live without you, but even as we breathed defiance, we knew that it was you who gave us breath to breathe. We pretended we were self-sufficient, but then we thought of accidents, disease, and death; and suddenly we understood afresh that we were only creatures set to spend a few brief years upon the earth and inexorably die. We cannot live without your power, Lord, nor die with even the slightest hope beyond the grave unless you exist and love and redeem. So we have come to church that we may worship you, that we may learn more about your will for us, and that we may better understand the meaning of our lives and more fully commit them to you.

We thank you for the good things we have known through your bounty and mercy: for the noble-hearted people who have so wrought themselves into our souls that we partook of their stature and were then stronger than we had ever thought we could be; for the incense of earth at the dawn of the day; for the rains of spring and the snows of winter; for seedtime and harvest and all the richness of the world that gives us food and drink and means of being warm and being clothed; for the chance to work and the time to rest; for fellowship with those of kindred mind; for music and books; for animals and flowers. We are so easily distraught, our Father, so prone to think that any pain is evil and any disappointment tragedy. We easily dwell only on what we lack and give no heed at all to treasures that are ours now and would be ardently coveted if not possessed. Set us then free, we beg you: free from the bondage of personal anguish and the menace of great world catastrophes. Convince us that the world is in your keeping, that anything possible is possible with you, that only truth is everlasting and only righteousness eternal.

Steer us into wide understanding, deep sympathies, broad tolerance. Spare us the shame of living only yesterday or only

tomorrow but never today. Teach us the desperate urgency of
now, and enable us to be honest today, to be kind today, to be
brave today. Send us into your service, Lord, or do not send us
anywhere. Grant us success in doing your will, or take us to
triumph through failure. In Jesus' name. *Amen.*

It Is Hard to Wait

It is hard for us to wait for you, our Father. Indeed, it is hard for us to wait for anyone or anything: hard to be patient, hard to be silent, hard to listen. There are so many words to be spoken—now! There are so many minds to be changed—now! There are so many wrongs to be righted—now! Apart from ourselves the world seems so blind and so deaf, so stupid and so evil that unless we run now, shout now, take control now, the creation that yesterday sang to your glory will tomorrow return to the void from which you once drew it.

Lord, could it be that you do not comprehend the urgencies of these times, that you have lived too long, that you have suffered too much, that you are weary and perhaps discouraged? We confess that we do not think of you often, but when we do, it is no lack of love that makes us sometimes want to seize the reins from your hands. Rather, we are troubled by your apparent bias toward procrastination, and there is too much at issue in these times to leave weighty decisions in hands not ready to take them.

So it is hard for us to wait for you, our Father. Hard, but still we need to ask you a question that shames us even in the asking of it. Could it be that we have no choice, or that our choices are only the worsening of chaos or the hardness of waiting? We hope that you will not misunderstand us: seeing the awful wickedness and knowing the horrible pain, we cannot *only* wait. We must act; we must protest; we must resist. We march, but where are we going? We make our proclamations, but what good do they accomplish? We long for light, but we often live in darkness. We hunger for reassurance, but many days are spent in despair. We dream of love, and we work for it; but we face much hatred, and we even help to beget it. Lord, what are we doing amiss? What is wrong in ourselves? Are you speaking to us, and have we failed to hear because we would not stop speaking to you?

It is hard for us to wait for you, our Father, but give us the wisdom still to wait—and the grace and the strength. Through Jesus Christ our Lord. *Amen.*

Origin of Everything That Has Been

Father, Son, and Holy Spirit, origin of everything that has been and destiny of all still to be, we go to you and meet you coming to us. Lord of our life and death, be known of us here, and grant that of this people none may seek your face in vain.

For the light already shed upon us we give you thanks: for the prophets of old who had no fear save fear of yourself, for the saints of the ages whose words became gates to your presence, for the record still kept in the Scripture we cherish and the faith still held in the church that we love. For the light already shed upon us we give you thanks.

For the sin that brings you pain we confess our guilt: for the waste of the bounty which you have provided, for the hatred that burns in the place of your love, for the warfare of people who were meant to be sisters and brothers, for the greed and the lust and the envy that, loathing in our peers, we allow in ourselves. For the sin that brings you pain we confess our guilt.

For your purpose in us we beg your triumph: that the prayers of our lips become the deeds of our lives, that there be neither prejudice nor arrogance in our quest of fulfillment, that neither weakness nor fear withhold us from shouldering our crosses. For your purpose in us we beg your triumph.

Father, you can do all things except compel the wills of your children. Confront us again and again with the love you revealed in your Son. Remind us how costly to you has been the toil of creation, how long and how wearying, how hard and how painful; and help us to handle with reverence a world brought into being by hands bloodied and calloused. We want to be people of faith. We want to be honest and brave and dependable. Teach us. Show us how. Through Jesus Christ our Lord. *Amen.*

For Universities and Other Schools

Eternal God, our heavenly Father, we have come to this place from places widespread and diverse. As spokes of a wheel we have lodged ourselves in the hub of our purpose, and the many now one, we lift one voice to acknowledge your lordship and put our trust in your care.

We pray for this school, potent both to be your witness and to be your burden. Grant that in strength it may be humble and in weakness unafraid, that in vision it may be pure and in blindness patient, that in safety it may be diligent and in danger steadfast for the truth.

We pray for those who sit here at the desks of decision. Save them alike from hardness of heart and from softness of head. Let not brittle chores make brittle those who do them, and on all entrusted with the order of this school's life bestow the light to be wise, the doggedness to persevere, and the grace to judge as those who know that they themselves are judged.

We pray for those who teach in these halls. Let them never cease to be students. So fill them with knowledge of yourself that they become translators of your handiwork, and so inflame them in their teaching that all facts are set aglow with your glory.

We pray for those who have come to learn from their teachers. Guard them both from expecting too little and from demanding too much. Permit them no patience with laziness or error in their teachers, but make bitter for them, too, all laziness and error in themselves. Save them from arrogance and envy, from greed and bad temper. Save them from the idleness that rots and from the zeal that consumes. Save them from saluting the givers of their grades and ignoring the parents in their homes.

We pray for those who hold in stewardship the humbler tasks of these houses and lands: those who plow the roads and cut the grass and plant the flowers, those who tend the fires and sweep the floors and dust the rooms, those who type the letters and make ready the mailings. In tribulation keep them calm, in need make them willing, and in work well done grant to them the joy of faithful colleagues. Deny them not the dignity of those whom you have called to share your purposes, and so quicken the consciences of all whose work they further that no needless burden may be laid upon them.

To your favor and grace, O Lord, we commend this school and all of its people. Let your benediction rest upon it, we pray; and bring forth from its halls fruits fit for your kingdom. Through Jesus Christ our Savior and Redeemer. *Amen.*

You Care for All Your People

Eternal Spirit, you care for all your people with love surpassing knowledge and would not willingly afflict any of your creatures with hardship or pain. We ask of you the strength and wisdom needed in the lives that you have given us. If we are young, preserve us alike from the insolence that flaunts the latest fad as arbiter of all and from the despair that thinks what always has been must ever still be. If we have come to the top of our probable climbing, not old and not young, but burdened with duties and overwhelmed by decisions, confound our self-pity and guard us from mourning too much the flight of our youth and fearing at all the advent of age. If death appears not to be distant, expel from our souls both complaint with the past and dread of the future. As long as we live, enable us to hamper none of your planning; empower us to further some of your purposes; enlighten us to comprehend more of your goodness and mercy.

Frustrate, O Lord, our separation of your two Great Commandments, and vouchsafe that loving you, we find our way quickly into love of our neighbors, and that loving our neighbors, we move no less swiftly into love of yourself. Imbue us with courage to love even our enemies. Feed us with conscience to count no human being a thing to be used. Break down the walls we build to protect our contentment. Force us to look at the scarred and the homeless, the cold and the hungry, and if you must withhold one blessing to bestow another, retain in your keeping the comfort we covet, and endow us instead with minds full of wisdom and hearts rich in compassion. Through Jesus Christ our Lord. *Amen.*

Help Our Unbelief

Spirit unseen, unheard, untouched, and undetectable by odor or taste, we believe in you; help our unbelief.

Assembled here in your presence, we are one body. From different homes and separate duties we come. Our purposes are past counting and our hopes as many as the members of this congregation. We do not always agree with one another, and it may even be that there are misunderstandings and resentments among us, rivalries and jealousies and enmities. Yet in this sacred house of prayer we stand on level ground; and conscious of hungers none but you can satisfy and humbled by sins none but you can forgive, we affirm that we are one: one in the search for your nature and being, one in the need of your mercy and love, one in the longing for your power and peace. Come then to each of us as each has need of you, and so uphold our noblest ambitions that going out at the end of our worship, we may be unencumbered henceforth by the doubts we have borne in our hearts to this place.

Grant, Lord, that we have no gods before you: not money or lands, not advancement in work or distinction at large, not comfort or safety or widespread approval. Suffer us to make no graven images of yourself, adoring the handiwork as if it were you; neither let us take your name in vain, parading ourselves in the counterfeited robes of your kingdom. Remind us of how much we ought to do but still have left undone, and gird us to make use of Sundays, public worship, fellowships of prayer, and all the other means whereby the human creatures of the earth discern that they are other creatures, too. Induce in us such esteem for the past that we pay due honor to fathers and mothers, and such regard for the present that we are freed from temptation to kill or steal or betray our loved ones in marriage. Spare us the guilt of bearing untrue witness to our neighbors, and rescue us from idle talk, distorted descriptions of innocent events, perverse attributions of thoughts never harbored or words never spoken. Fill us at last with such gratitude to you for your gifts to ourselves that we need not covet your gifts to our sisters and brothers, and to you be the glory forever. *Amen.*

SPECIAL OCCASIONS

First Sunday in Advent

God Almighty, Father of our Lord Jesus Christ and our Father, and Holy Spirit always beyond us but ever within, to you in the highest be all glory and praise! We walk in darkness, but we have seen a great light. We dwell in the land of the shadow of death, but upon us the bright flame has descended. How good are your tidings, how great their joy!

Yet how silent of old was the coming of your Son—how unforeseen in Bethlehem was the King foretold by the seers, how incongruous at Nazareth was the Prince of Peace extolled by the prophets. You are so often courteous in your insistence, tender in your mightiness, patient in your thunder. Are you to come again in these days of Advent, or have you come already and come again in such stealth that we have not seen or not understood what we saw?

Keep us awake, we beseech you, alert for signs of your holy intrusions. Open our minds, unseal our hearts, unclench our souls, and suffuse our bodies with strength sufficient for the unexpected burdens of your nearness; and should a lowly place be once again the site of your lodging, grant us not to be blind to your splendor or deaf to your pleading.

Lord, have mercy on us for the sparseness of substance that locks out the hurts of your people around us, for the coldness of being that feels not the cold of our sisters and brothers, for the corruption of spirit that repulses the knock of the needy. Preserve us from such reluctance to pity that we become ourselves pitiful. Let not cheapness in loving turn our whole lives into cheapness. Extend our perceptions, enlarge our affections, and so prepare us for the manger that we are ready for the cross. Through Jesus Christ our Lord. *Amen.*

Second Sunday in Advent

Omnipotent, omniscient, and infinite God, King of kings and Lord of lords, once again we come to the time of the coming of Jesus, and again we make ready our hearts to receive him. We remember in awe your wondrous gift at the manger, and beholding anew that night in the stable, we praise and bless your holy name.

For shepherds in the fields abiding, lowly men, no doubt, and roughly hewn, humble in the angels' glory, hastening to see the newborn baby and returning to their sheep with adoration of you for all that they had heard and seen—for the shepherds in the fields abiding we praise and bless your holy name.

For the wise men from the East, beholding the star and coming to worship, finding the child and in amazement rejoicing, opening their treasures and bestowing their gifts, owning the King who transcended their kingships—for the wise men from the East we praise and bless your holy name.

For Joseph, the carpenter of Nazareth, comprehending in part but only in part the stupendous events through which he was passing, loving his Mary and loving his Jesus, wanting only to do what was needed, seeking no more than to do what was right—for Joseph the carpenter of Nazareth we praise and bless your holy name.

For Mary, the mother of Jesus, virgin betrothed to the carpenter Joseph and hailed by the angel to be the matrix of Jesus, meekly submitting and bravely bearing, keeping always the strange night in her heart and pondering, pondering, pondering—for Mary the mother of Jesus we praise and bless your holy name.

More than the others, for Jesus himself, the child born to be King, the boy reared in the home of the carpenter, the teacher and healer, the friend and companion, the man on the cross and the Savior of all—for Jesus himself we praise and bless your holy name, and we pray that through these days of Advent we may be drawn ever closer to him and to you. *Amen.*

Third Sunday in Advent

Forgive us, Lord, our paltry preparations for Christmas. Before the summer has ended, we have started the wearying process: reading the catalogs, ordering the cards, listing the presents, buying the wrappings. As winter approaches and the cold descends, the pace quickens, the chaos engulfs, the tempers flare, the great day appears and is gone, and exhaustion ensues. And in the season of Advent we have made ready for all but *the advent.*

If never before and never again, save us this year from repeating the endless repetitions. Resolutely, ruthlessly, relentlessly—let us put out of our lives the hurrying and the scurrying, the hasting and the wasting, the huffing and the puffing. Calm us down. Cool us off. Shut us up. Compel us to stop, to be quiet, still, silent. Then turn us around. Alter our perceptions; change our direction.

Is not your Son the meaning of Christmas, our Father? Is not his the birthday we celebrate, his the glory we sing, his the life we pledge ourselves to emulate? Prepare us then to receive again from your hands the gift beyond all other giving. Prevent us not understanding the immensity of Christmas, the majesty, the grandeur, the inextricable intertwining with all things cosmic and universal, all things endless and eternal. If never before and never again, help us this year to lift up our eyes to yourself, to strive to be perfect as you yourself are perfect, to do justly and love mercy and walk humbly where you lead us. If never before and never again, help us this year to honor the Prince of Peace by becoming ourselves peacemakers. If never before and never again, help us this year to make room in our inns for the Christ in our brothers and sisters: persuade us to offer food to the hungry and drink to the thirsty; open our hearts to the homeless, the lonely, the imprisoned. In Jesus' name. *Amen.*

Fourth Sunday in Advent

Mighty God and Merciful Father, how swiftly pass the days before the day of celebration! For months we prepare for the birthday of your Son—look forward to it, long for it, dream about its wonderful beauty and warmth. Then suddenly it has come and is passed, and we have not felt what we wanted to feel, not been what we wanted to be.

Not quite too late for this year, it yet is not early, and we pray, Lord, that you will so enliven within us the true love of your Son that we offer ourselves to be gifts at his manger. Inasmuch as we do it to one of the least of his kindred, we do it also to him, he has told us. Disengage us then from the tinsel and baubles, the colored lights and candies and turkey, and aid us to be just: telling the truth to people we like or we don't, returning full measure for all payments received, acknowledging guilt when incurred and extending at once our full restitution. Assist us to be kind: repudiating any sort of hatred and all forms of malice, raising the fallen and defending the wounded, leading the lost and feeding the hungry. Help us to be brave: not withered by laughter or frightened by scorn, not silenced by threats or routed by anger, not open to bribes and not offered for sale. Enable us to be Christlike: doing our duty and then doing more, bearing our burdens and then bearing our crosses, loving our friends and then loving our enemies, denying ourselves and then laying down our lives.

As we paint our pictures of Christmas, let us not overdo the pastels, our Father—the gentle blues and golds of the fairy tales and the children's books. Save us room, too, for the full black and the white, the deep red and the orange. For the child in the manger was the man on the cross, and our struggle, like his, confronts the power of evil in high places, the armies of wickedness in great numbers, genocide and massacre and war, starvation and betrayal and torture, murder and arson and rape. Take not away the toys from our children, but preserve us ourselves from toying with Christmas. Keep us strong for its wars. Make us pure for its battles. Through Jesus Christ our Lord. *Amen.*

Christmas

God almighty, God eternal, who brooded of old upon the chaos and out of the chaos brought forth order and in the order planned a place where humankind might dwell in love and peace, we thank you that in the fullness of time you made flesh your Word in Jesus Christ.

Year by ending year we turn again toward Bethlehem. In the night we seek the star that then the wise men followed, and we long to stand at last where once the shepherds stood and hear again the songs that once the angels sang. So dark the skies now seem above us, Lord, so frightening the tumult round about— the wars and the menace of wars; the distrust and the hatred; the corruption and the violence; the greed and the lechery and the waste and the fear; the hunger and the homelessness and the disease and the pain. Despair is so easy, and hope is so hard. It is so tempting to surrender, so tiring to fight on.

Yet ever we know that skies now dark were dark as well for Joseph and Mary, and that glory manifested once to hearts humble to receive it waits now for hearts prepared to welcome its return. Who would have thought that you would choose a stable for your coming or that manger hay would prove a cradle for the King of kings and Lord of lords? How many, seeing then, believed? How many, hearing, lent their credence to the heard?

Are we still as blind today, our Father, still as deaf? Still do we look for signs of your coming where Herod rules and seek your presence in the halls where Caiaphas presides? Are swords more dear to us than plowshares? Have we any gods above our banks and our brokers? When was it last we fed the hungry, gave drink to the thirsty, sheltered strangers, clothed the naked, visited the sick, or went to those in prison?

Grant us peace in this Christmastide, our Father, for minds distraught are not minds apt for your calling. But being peaceful, may we not be complacent. Imbue us with your own abhorrence of the wrongs that surround us. Recruit us for your own attacks on the evils holding their sway among us. When the advent is over and the day of the birth is past and done, we would not be numbered with the proud whom you have scattered in the imagination of their hearts, nor with the mighty whom you have put down from their seats, nor with the rich whom you have sent away empty. We would be found among your servants who have fought the good fight and finished their course and kept the faith. Through Jesus Christ our Lord. *Amen.*

Sunday After Christmas

Now it is over, our Father. The long-awaited day of rejoicing is ended. Another year must pass before we celebrate again the birthday of Jesus, and we confess that some of us are weary and some of us fretful and some simply depressed. Terminations of glory are seldom uplifting. Beginnings are more happy than endings.

Yet is not a birth a beginning, Lord? A start, not a finish? Hailing the birth of your Son, do we not commemorate a life that was to mature in wisdom and stature until it embraced the whole globe with its love and its power; and is not then our own observance a commencement, not a conclusion? Swing us around, we pray. Turn us from looking backward with sorrow as of parting, and face us ahead with joy as of meeting. Let us ponder the past in our hearts as did Mary, but only that we feed on its fruits in the days still before us. Grant that we return to our everyday tasks like the shepherds—glorifying and praising you for all that we have seen and heard. Grant that we leave the stable behind us like the wise men—going back to our regular chores by a different way.

What are we to learn from Christmas, our Father? Certainly that your strength is made perfect in weakness and that you are never more perfectly present than when some would say you are not present at all. Surely also that you are not too busy still to care about our own tiny planet, that you have not abandoned your people to the offspring of their sins, and that your love remains more mighty than the might of all the evil round about us. Confound us then if we wallow in self-pity. Oppose our temptation to say that nothing matters and that nothing can be done to change what has been. Stir us out of lethargy. Prod us into labor. Lead us into the joy of doing the good within reach: what we can, where we can, when we can. Born your children, we have pledged ourselves to be disciples of your Son, Jesus Christ. Hold us, we pray, to our pledges. In Jesus' name. *Amen.*

New Year's Day

Lord God of all ages and peoples, from whom at first we came, to whom at last we go, and in whom we now live on the earth, we turn our thought to you as another year begins.

Young or old, all of us are old—stiffened by habit, blinded by prejudice, deafened by greed, crippled by sin—and we pray that you, who can make all things new, will effect in us new birth, new faith, new hope. The decades have passed, and from this church have gone unnumbered men and women to be disciples of your Son and priests in the priesthood of all believers. Sometimes you doubtless found in them another body, responsive to your bidding and attentive to your will; and sometimes you must have found in them another burden, a stumbling block, a cross. Of our own weaknesses we already know many, our Father, and we ask of you both forgiveness and redemption. Others of them we suspect that we do not yet recognize, and we pray that you will lead us into such knowledge of self that we discover how sorely we need your guidance and cleansing. Frail in ourselves, we are mighty in you; and in the year now opening before us, we beg that you will save us from thinking privilege a right to be hoarded, from being parasites either on past or on present, from wasting the hours the infirm would count precious.

Subject us to discipline. Step by urgent step grow us into faithful husbands and wives, diligent fathers and mothers, helpful citizens; nurture us to be loyal sons and daughters, honest workers, warmhearted Christians. Beget in us the hunger to be unobtrusively but incorruptibly good—truthful, kind, trustworthy, generous, forgiving. Draw us ever closer to yourself; plant our feet ever more firmly in the footsteps of Jesus. In arrogance defeat us; in despair give us hope. At midnight or noon enable us to fight the good fight; empower us to finish the course. Through Jesus Christ our Lord. *Amen.*

Epiphany

God Almighty, Spirit Eternal, without whom is nothing and beyond whom nowhere, we call to remembrance in worship the coming of the Magi to the manger. Would that we ourselves had found more stars to follow! Would that finding the few, we had mustered our courage and followed!

We thank you for not being narrow, provincial, bigoted. We thank you for not loving one race or religion or people and ignoring all of the others. We thank you that in the manifestation of your Son in the stable there was room at the manger for the wise men as well as the shepherds, for the Gentiles as well as the Jews, for the rich as well as the poor, for the scholars as well as the laborers, for the strangers as well as the neighbors. Did you not proclaim in the Magi that the gospel has no limits and no boundaries, no walls and no fences? Did you not declare in the Magi that no one is excluded from the rule of your Son, that he blesses and judges without favor or fawning, and that one day at last he shall reign and prevail, the King of all kings and the Lord of all lords?

You have called us in the church to be a new body for Christ, and we pray that you will enable us to carry his living spirit into all of the world. Beget in us a thirst to discover the meaning of his life in every pursuit of our work and our play: in schools and hospitals, in factories and churches, in prisons and stores, in homes and banks, on bombers and cruise ships. Teach us yourself that we ourselves may teach. Help us to find doors in blank walls of resistance, to commend piety without seeming pompously pious, to overcome embarrassment in speaking about things more important than all other things. Make us strong that we may offer strength; make us wise that we may communicate wisdom; make us good that we may not do harm to our sisters and brothers. Through Jesus Christ our Lord. *Amen.*

Race Relations Sunday

Creator God and sovereign Lord, you who still create and still hold sway, we praise you for the wonderful versatility of your creation: for the birds of the air and the beasts of the field and the fish of the sea, for trees and flowers and vegetables, for sky and clouds and snow and rain, and especially now for the intriguing diversity of your human begetting. How dull humanity would be without the colors, our Father, without the differences, with nothing but sameness, nothing but duplicates! How utterly painful the days would become if I never saw anything except me!

So we beg your forgiveness that so often we have censured your providence, found it unsettling that we were not your exclusive designs, resented our brothers and sisters for shades and shapes in their bodies that they could choose or reject no more than ourselves. Uphold in your love, we pray, all who suffer hurt or deprivation because of the race with which you have clothed them. Save them from responding to hatred with hatred, from turning bitter in the bitterness that engulfs them, from succumbing to despair when nothing they do seems to make any difference. Discourage in ourselves the sin of not caring—the deception that not being against the oppressed, we are for them; the insecurity that makes us want always to have somebody else behind or beneath us; the mistake that the wrongs not corrected today cannot hurt us tomorrow.

Enroll all of the races in symphony unlimited, and teach us to perform in tune and perform together. Enlist all of the races in army unbounded, and train us to march in step and march straight forward. We would be one in the passage, one in the journey. Through Jesus Christ our Lord. *Amen.*

Martin Luther King, Jr., Day

Almighty and eternal Father, giver of all that is given and maker of all that is made, we know that you love all of your people with an everlasting love and care for each with care beyond ending. You do not change, and have been the same from the earliest moment until now and will remain unaltered though the earth be removed and the place of humankind's home be no more. Recalling our gratitude for Martin Luther King, Jr., we turn to you because from you he came in the beginning, and in your hand he still abides.

We cannot forget the anguish and the anger with which we heard that he was dead. So suddenly we were catapulted to the edge of the unwanted abyss. There was so much we did not know about the days ahead; there was so much we did not know about our own hearts. But even in the darkness we were not left without light, and if there was much we did not know, there was much we did. We knew that however bad the world might be in spite of Martin Luther King, Jr., it was immeasurably better because of him. We knew that no matter who had pulled the trigger that killed him, there was scarcely one among us who had not played a little part in fashioning the gun and the bullet. We knew that Martin Luther King, Jr., had sought justice for his people in a land washed clean of prejudice and hatred, of poverty and hunger, of fear and contention. And we knew that nothing could more swiftly violate the dream for which he died than the violence that leapt so swiftly from his death.

Save us from cowardice, our Father; save us from weakness. Deny us the comfort of saying that the loss of our leader has brought the end of our cause, that we do not know what road to take or what load to carry. The promised land is still before us, and the path is clear beyond the Jordan. We have seen the footsteps pointing toward Jerusalem, and the word returns as once it did of old: "If any man would come after me, let him deny himself and take up his cross and follow me." We cannot claim the bliss of ignorance, and we pray that you will forgive us the sin that in every act of hatred or indifference we have known or had the means of knowing what we did. Chasten us,

Lord; cleanse us; save us; and make us such instruments of your powerful grace that within the narrow borders of our own little strength the death which came too early may not have come too late. Through Jesus Christ our Lord. *Amen.*

Ash Wednesday

Eternal God, Master of all things and all people, Father of our Lord Jesus Christ, as Lent begins, we call to remembrance the ending of Christmas. How wonderful the days of Advent! How glorious the time of the birth! How proper then to be kind, how right to be generous and merciful and loving; how easy to slip the harsh bonds of the past and live henceforth in freedom from all of the wrongs that enchained us!

Now Christmas long since has been over. The weeks have passed into months; our dreams have disappeared in their passage; and we confess to you in penitence that we are not what we wanted to be, nor where. So many things we have left undone: the kind words to husband or wife; the time spent with children; the gifts to victims of flood and drought, of war and rebellion; the cards of sympathy and the letters of congratulation and the telephone calls of inquiry; the care for the aged and the food provided in illness; the tasks of the church and the school and the hospital. So many things we have left undone, and so many things we have done: spoken when we ought to have kept silent; kept silent when we ought to have spoken; betrayed trust; told lies; broken pledges; stolen from stores; driven while drunk; committed adultery; harbored grudges; nursed hatreds; sought vengeance; started quarrels.

Forgive us, Lord. Although we knew what we were doing and still did it, forgive us, and so tend us through the Lenten weeks that we truly repent us of our sins, are in love and charity with our neighbors, and lead a new life. Make us ready for the upper room. Prepare us for the cross. Equip us for an Easter morning. Hear us, we beseech you; for we would be faithful disciples of your Son, Jesus Christ, and in his name we pray. *Amen.*

Palm Sunday

Father of Jesus Christ and our Father, whose eye is on the sparrow's flight and who care even for the lilies of the field, how poignant for you must have been the passage of your Son through the gates of Jerusalem: the freedom so soon to be bondage, the life to be lost so quickly in death. We summon to memory his love and his courage, his alertness to duty and allegiance to you. We recreate in our minds the ride on the donkey, the crowds in their tumult, the waving of palms, and the shouted hosannas. We see looming before him the decision of Pilate and the end on the cross.

Teach us, Lord, the lessons in those days of glory, days of sadness. We would not withhold adoration from Jesus, not sit on our hands while the King of all kings is marching in splendor; but neither would we hail him in safety and desert him in danger, not praise him on Sunday and on Friday call, "Crucify!" Keep sober our promises and honest our pledges. Bolt fast the word to the act, and prevent the assumption that a good deed considered is a benefaction completed. So often we stand at the gate and cheer, and still stand at the gate when the cheering has stopped. Take us all the way. Take us all the way with the man on the donkey. Through the casting out of the moneychangers in the temple and the long conversations with all who would listen, through the body and blood of the dark upper room and the still darker dark of Gethsemane's prayer, through the fury of Caiaphas and the judgment of Pilate and the hammer and nails of Golgotha take us all the way to the cross. Turn into flesh the faith that is in us. Incarnate our noble intentions. Break open the vaults wherein we have stored our commitment as Christians, and deny us contentment in transcending our Sundays only at weddings and funerals.

Grant that believing at Bethlehem's stable, we believe no less bravely at Jerusalem's cross, that being faithful in worship, we bear witness as truly at work and at play. Through Jesus Christ our Lord. *Amen.*

Maundy Thursday

Almighty God, Creator ever creating, Father still begetting, hear us as we come again to the holy table and remember the upper room. Who are we, Lord? Are we Peter, soon to deny but at last to stand firm? Are we James and John, competing for seats at the right and the left of the heavenly throne? Are we Andrew or Philip, Bartholomew or Simon, less known than some others but still longing to serve? Or are we even perhaps the one on the edge of betraying, and is the question you need from us "Lord, is it I?"

You know what stumbling blocks we have set before us as we struggled toward your face. We have sought you with minds but not hearts; we have praised you with lips but not lives. We have said that we wanted nothing more than sight of yourself but then so befogged our souls with sinning that far from seeing what we said we were seeking, we could not see anything right or anything true. We have prayed for your coming but been at once so afraid that our prayers might be answered that we bolted our doors against the possibility.

Break the doors down, we beseech you. Cleanse us of pride that corrupts and destroys. Avert the doubtfulness that masks itself with arrogance. Deliver us from such preoccupation with pulling at our own bootstraps that we have no hand to give you when you lean to help us. We are often stubborn, often stiff-necked, often fearful, lest losing our lives to Christ, we can never retrieve them. Reconvince us of your power. Reassure us of your love. Allow us no comfort in the thunder of evil, but permit us no trembling. Set us free from every enslavement both to self and to others, and grant that standing at last in the liberty wherewith you endowed us, we may not shed our burdens and not shirk our crosses. Through Jesus Christ our Lord. *Amen.*

Good Friday

Save us, our Father, from enjoying ourselves with the cross. Do you laugh or do you cry as you watch us adorning ourselves with its gold reproductions? Was it not a tool for the infliction of torture, an instrument for the dealing of death? Should not only they wear it who are willing to bear it? Incline us then to don our crosses with sad recollections and guilty reflections—always as badges, always as pledges, always as public declaration of private commitment. And spare us the shame of professing the faith we have no intention to practice.

Reveal to us, we pray, the multiple meanings of this day and its death: the sheer horror of wickedness unconstrained in its power; the ineffable beauty of life unconquered by terror, uncorrupted by hatred, untrammeled by self; the extravagant cost of creation and the price you have paid for our birth and our rearing; the solemn digestion of tragedy and the ultimate impotence of wrong before the meek perseverance of right. Chasten our wish that we were better than we are: more true and more just, more kind and more generous, more patient and more forgiving. Deny us escape by digging for the roots of our failures in somebody else's garden. We would prefer to blame our failures on inheritance of temper from father or mother, provocation beyond endurance from neighbors or friends, stupidity of clerks or collapses of banks or bad spells of weather. Turn us inward, and then turn us outward. Induce us to accept accountability for the persons we are and the ones we can be, and then give us no peace until we offer our lives to further your will.

Enable us to make the little choices that shape the big decisions, to do good deeds to those without power to help us, to carry burdens of righteousness with no righteous obligation to carry them. We cannot be Christ, but we long to be like him. Empower us then to follow where he leads us—even to Jerusalem, even to Calvary, even to the cross. *Amen.*

Easter

Almighty God, eternal Spirit, who raised from the dead our Lord Jesus Christ and pledged through his resurrection that they who died with him for your sake would live with him by your power, we praise you for this holy day, and we thank you for its witness to your care for your people.

That we have sinned you know, our Father. That we have been blind to your glory and deaf to your pleading you know, our Father. That we have been weak when we could have been strong, cruel when we should have been kind, stingy when we had the means to be generous, and cowardly when we had cause to be brave you know, our Father. For the evil done and the good not done we ask your forgiveness, and again we praise you for this holy day and thank you for its witness to your care for your people.

Hear us as we pray for all sorts and conditions of your human creatures: the proud who have no reason for pride and the shamed who are more victims of wrong than its doers; men and women with power; children of privilege; adults afraid and trembling; children starving and naked; Jews and Arabs; Catholics and Protestants; Buddhists and Moslems; the lonely and the bitter; the insane and the imprisoned; the sick and the wounded and the dying; those who have lost their fortunes and those who have lost their loved ones and those who have lost their hope. You removed from wicked men their victory at Calvary and denied the tomb its prisoner in Joseph's garden; come again as you have promised, and have mercy on the humankind of your creation.

Invade, we pray, the lands that we have walled against you. Breach the fortresses that we have built to exclude you. Whether by raising or by lowering, whether by empowering or by enfeebling, whether by giving or by refraining from giving— extend to all of us the ministries we need.

Wanting peace, we have made war. Seeking friends, we have raised up foes. Coveting goodness, we have grown spiteful and prejudiced and wretched. You can do all things, and we pray that you will do for us what we have not been able to do for ourselves. Save us, our Father. Save us from our friends. Save us from our enemies. Save us from ourselves. Through Jesus Christ our Lord. *Amen.*

Family Sunday

God almighty, Father eternal, who deemed it not good that any of your children be lonely and who ordained the family to be a shelter for love and fulfillment, we come to you in prayer for our nearest and dearest. While silently we share with you our deepest concerns and desires, return your answer, Lord, as may be most expedient for those we now commend to your care.

One by one, but still in common need and hope, let us pray for our homes. Let us name in our hearts the ones who share with us the daily events and resources, and let us thank God for their blessed ministry of support and compassion.

Let us pray that our homes may be more than locations of residence and greater than bases of livelihood. Let us ask that the spirit of God enter their doors and abide in their rooms, touching each relationship with God's glory and uniting all family members in pursuit of the good and the true.

Let us pray for those who belong to our homes but are not with us now, those cleft from us by distance or misunderstanding, those separated from us by the duties of education or breadwinning labor. Let us pray that they may be strong in the day of need, brave in the hour of danger, and faithful in the time of testing.

Let us pray especially for our mothers, those long since departed from the earth and those still living among us. Let us thank God for all the good and faithful in their number, remembering before God their patient love, their ceaseless travail, and their unconquerable hope.

Let us pray for all the homes in the world: broken homes whence love has long ago disappeared, diminished homes where death has stalked and stolen, anxious homes where fear is rampant, hungry homes where jobs have been lost and funds exhausted. Let us pray that God will speed the time when all of God's people dwell at peace in their own households and walk in trust with those they love.

Receive our prayers, Lord—those heard by all of us and those others heard only by yourself. Receive and answer in Jesus' name. *Amen.*

Pentecost

Almighty God, who called us in the church to be a body for your Son, Jesus Christ, enliven that body, we pray. Quicken in us the will to do what Jesus himself instructed, and grant us wisdom and power for all that we do in his name.

From lives widely different and tasks diverse we have come to this place for our worship, and we shall go back to those tasks and those lives when our worship is ended. Encourage us to preach as we go—not necessarily from pulpits or platforms, but by word or by deed making known in the world what wonderful changes faith has made in our living. Enable us to heal the sick, perhaps not by the laying on of hands or dispensing of remedies, but through wholesome and healthy interaction, giving strength to the ill in their weakness. Teach us to cleanse the lepers, probably not that we shall encounter any actual leprosy, but by open and friendly approaches, welcoming home to their humanness the despised, the outcast, the rejected. Arm us to raise the dead, not by exhuming bodies or breaking down doors in the tombs, but through so allowing ourselves to be filled with your spirit that we summon back into life the souls who have died in their boredom, their fear, or their sin. Commission us to cast out demons, not through the working of magic on troublesome Satans, but by the humble submission of ourselves to your purpose, offering you tools for the purging of guilt and jealousy, of hatred and lust and despair.

Lord, we cannot ask for a sound from heaven like the rush of the mighty wind that filled all the house at the first Pentecost of our faith, not for tongues as of fire distributed and resting on each one of us. Enough for this people if you so pour out your Spirit upon us that our young see visions, our old dream dreams, and our sons and our daughters discover ever new words to proclaim the good news of your love. Awaken this church, we beseech you, and keep it unsleeping. Sanctify it, and maintain it unsullied. Recruit it to your service, and hold it unfailing. Through Jesus Christ our Lord. *Amen.*

Memorial Day

Lord of all times and all places, all things and all people, do we spend too many of our days in the future—devising and planning, reaching and straining, hoping and dreading? Have we forgotten too often our debts to the past? Today in your presence we turn our thoughts backward and call to remembrance the days that have been.

We remember our fathers and mothers and all who before them helped to fashion the beings we turned out to be. For their frailties we can only have sympathy; shall we not bestow weakness ourselves on our sons and our daughters? We publish our thanks for their strength and their succor, their kindness and caring, their loving and sharing, their persuading and guiding.

We remember the birth of this nation and the noblest aspiring of the ones who begot it. For all its departures from truth, justice, and merciful governance, we entreat your forgiveness, and we pray for your aid in its search for redemption. Encourage when deserved; chasten where needed; and in all things restore and renew to your glory.

We remember all who have fought for their country: combatants in war who hated the killing and longed only for peace, conscientious objectors who wanted less to object than to serve peace as its makers. All honor and praise to conscience and duty; all praise and full honor to the brave and the true.

We remember in pity the vast unremembered: the victims of war and rebellion, of harassment and torture, of drought and starvation, of racial persecution and religious oppression. Move us here to intervene and defend, to uplift and uphold, and hasten the day when all of your children will dwell together at peace in the house of their Father.

Lord of all times and all places, all things and all people, we have turned our thoughts backward and called to remembrance the days that have been. As we turn them now forward to the days still to be, deny us ignoring, prevent us forgetting. Through Jesus Christ our Lord. *Amen.*

Children's Day

Father of all, from whom we came at the beginning, in whose family we remain always full members and by whom we are taken at last to life beyond our present conceiving, we pray for all children.

We call to mind in your hearing the sheer wonder of childhood when viewed by adults: the incredible blendings of deception and innocence, beauty and ugliness, mercy and vengeance, suspicion and trust. We consider the children themselves and try to remember how we felt when we stood in their places: the strange interminglings of sadness and joy, the demanding of freedom and the fright at its prospect, the wanting to know and the dread of finding out, the slow pacing of time and the impatience in waiting, the vulnerability in pain and the sensitivity to ridicule.

Keep us, Lord, from hurting any child. If we cannot do good, withhold us at least from damage. Lead us on the path of honest inquiry, and spare us the guilt of assuming that anything untried must be something unworthy. In awkward beginnings help us discern the stuff of fine endings. Guide us to interpret rightly the conduct otherwise reprehensible: the insecurity that hides itself in surliness, the desperate need to be noticed that bursts out in brashness, the searching for selfhood that leads into dark pits and blind alleys. Let us not treat with contempt the pain of maturing: trying to play fairly while surrounded by cheating, hunting for heroes in the confusion of villains, hungering for answers and starving on silence. Save us alike from expecting too much and too little, from destroying one talent in the mold for another, from recreating ourselves in our sons and our daughters, from demanding the what but not explaining the how.

We pray for all children, our Father. Sustain them in strength and uphold them in weakness. From danger protect, and from temptation defend. Shed light in their darkness; establish peace in their tumult; bless them with joy in their sadness; and everywhere and always lead them closer to yourself. Through Jesus Christ our Lord. *Amen.*

Independence Day

God of all places and peoples, to whom no one is an alien nor any a stranger, we commemorate in worship the birth of this our well-beloved nation, and we celebrate the independence it won through struggle and hardship. Here in your presence we acknowledge our debt to our fathers and mothers and to the long succession of mothers and fathers before them who hungered for liberty and thirsted for freedom and left behind them for us the rich fruits of their labors. It is good to be free, to do what we want and go where we please; we would not live elsewhere nor be lured into bondage.

Yet are there no perils, our Father, for a nation so mighty and a people so strong? Does not power still corrupt and absolute power corrupt absolutely? Let it not be too easy for us to get our own way, to rattle our sabers and frighten the world to submission. Restrain us from bluster and bombast, from rhetoric unbonded to truth and achievement, from dissemblance of justice and pretensions of virtue. Disturb the complacency wherewith we interpret good fortune as the proof of our goodness. Dissuade us from hoarding unneeded resources without which our neighbors are dying. Preserve us from softness of head and hardness of heart, from thinking that any can be safe until all have been saved, and from wanting all to be safe for no better reason than ourselves being saved.

Of us to whom so much has been given require as abundantly, Lord. Induce us, being rich in possessing, to be equally profuse in dispersing. Discontent us with all except excellence: in science and art, in education and religion, in sheltering and feeding, in healing and caring. Temper always our might with mercy; keep us, whenever most sure, most surely prepared to be taught; and whatever we do, let all be done as by sons and daughters of the Father eternal. Through Jesus Christ our Lord. *Amen.*

Labor Day

Creator God and first of all workers, we acknowledge in worship the toil you have spent in the world of our living, and we ask your blessing on all who labor for the good of the earth and the welfare of people.

We pray for all workers who are bored with their work, endlessly repeating repetitive tasks that need to be done but offer no joy in their doing. Hasten the day when other means will be found for their duties and better use will be made of their talents, and grant that meanwhile they conceive all of their separate motions as individual services rendered to unknown but particular persons.

We pray for all workers who may never outlive the maturation of effort: counselors counseling, teachers teaching, ministers ministering; foresters planting trees, scientists launching experiments, builders erecting cathedrals. Embrace in their care the length and the breadth of your planning and shaping, and end not their joy with the end of their seeing.

We pray for all workers whose tasks are often hard and unpleasant: the plowing of roads and the digging of ditches, the cleaning of sewers and the collecting of garbage, the nursing of the sick and the burial of the dead. Sustain them in dignity; keep firm in their thinking the worth of their labor; and grant them due pride that so much of life's process proceeds on their shoulders.

We pray for all workers apparently workless: the crippled and broken, the sick and the dying, the cast out and rejected. Kindle in them the awareness that many a battle is fought on a sickbed, that many hard tasks are performed on our backs, that worth is not established by graphs and statistics, that the noblest achievement is often a smile.

These and all other workers we commend to your keeping, our Father. Imbue them with strength, we pray. Instill in them wisdom; correct their follies; forgive their sins; and endow them with true faith in our Lord Jesus Christ. *Amen.*

Reformation Sunday

God Almighty, you who never were not and always will be, Father of our Lord Jesus Christ, and Holy Spirit now present among us, we commend for your blessing the church called forth by your Son. We confess to you in shame how far we have fallen from grace in its service, and we praise you that, often reformed, it is ever reforming.

You have summoned us to be priests in the priesthood of all who believe, and we would open faith's doors for our sisters and brothers; but let us not be too proud to walk through the doors held open by them for ourselves. We would be doers of the Word and not hearers only, but keep us ever mindful that it is you who can save and none other and that the works of our hands are the fruits of our faith, not its substance.

We call to remembrance the church in its early beginnings, the frightened disciples abounding in courage, standing fast in their trembling, speaking out in their fear. We remember the church in its youthful maturing, now good and now bad, now strong and now weak, now right and now wrong, but never quite conquered, never quite lost. We follow the church through its prideful dominion: its flickers of light in the abyss of its darkness, its saints still begotten in the womb of its sinning, its painters and carvers still carving and painting the beauty that taunted the taste of their sponsors, its scholars still defending their knowledge against assaults by the witless, its healers still tender among the brutes and the savages. And we think of the church reborn and renewed: the valiant protestors who recalled it to glory and infused it with power, the reliable witnesses who rediscovered your gospel and published abroad what they found.

How lengthy the line that stretches behind us, our Father. How wondrous the roll of faith's mothers and fathers! Let us not handle lightly the treasure and talent. Has not blood been spilled to our benefit? Have not lives been lost for our sake? Through Jesus Christ our Lord. *Amen.*

World Community Day

Almighty and eternal God, who in the beginning created the heaven and the earth and brought forth order from chaos when the earth was without form and void, and darkness was upon the face of the deep—out of chaos again bring order, we pray. The uproar encircles our world and engulfs it. How can we sow justice in anarchy; how grow peace or beauty or kindness? Once more then we ask for your own intervention: out of the chaos bring order, bring order, bring order.

Yet did you not beget us to be people—neither puppets nor slaves; and how can you coerce the very wills you endowed with the right to resist you; and if order is prerequisite to justice, is not justice to order? So we alter our prayer to beseech you: accept us as your heralds, stewards, and agents; and equip us to work the just works that build order from chaos.

There is so much we could do but have not. Could we not be more just ourselves—more truthful, more honest, more worthy of trust and dependence? Have we assumed available roles in the orderly pursuits of our neighborhoods? Could we not break silence about issues affecting the right and the good, contribute our own little weight to brave leaders in places of power, prepare for tomorrow the foundations of honor today?

Lord, we remember with particular sorrow the victims of degradation and oppression, of neglect and rejection, of torment and torture. Keep alive in our hearts their hurt and their anguish, their cold and their hunger, their despair and their loneliness. Make sleepless our nights of uncaring; unclench the fists that hold back the help we could proffer; and move closer the day when the one world of your building will be one in living, when all of earth's people will dwell together in love and at peace, one family praising and blessing their Father in heaven. Through Jesus Christ our Lord. *Amen.*

Thanksgiving

It is not easy to give thanks, our Father. Not because we have so few blessings for which to be grateful, but because we have so many. Many of our prayers seem to be praising you because we are not like so many other people—not hungry or cold, not homeless or lonely—and then we feel guilty and find it less painful to stop all our praising and thanking.

Yet how can we fail to acknowledge the marvelous bounty with which you endow your human creation? Things too far for our sight and too small for our seeing, colors more varied than words can encompass and fragrances sweet beyond all description, music that carries the soul into heavenly mansions, food overflowing for all of your people and water that sings as it sparkles its way through the valleys, beasts in the fields and birds in the air and fish in the oceans, children and friends and more loved ones, work to be done and games to be played, books to be read and mountains to be climbed and seas to be crossed—how incredible your providence, how inconceivable your diversity, how incomprehensible your abundance, how unimaginable your generosity!

Yet how twisted and faulty our own responding! We have deliberately damaged our brothers and sisters. We have coveted, hated, lusted, and envied. We have imprisoned the innocent, persecuted the righteous, and made war on the helpless. We have lied and stolen and perverted and starved. We have polluted resources bequeathed to us clean. We have hugged to ourselves wealth meant to be shared. We have destroyed and vandalized, wasted and squandered. And our sin is the greater because we are not unequipped with mental capacity. You have given us brains; we could know what we do.

Lord, forgive us, we pray. Although we do not deserve it, forgive us. Accept our tainted thanksgiving; enliven our dawning repentance; and set our feet on the way we should go. Through Jesus Christ our Lord. *Amen.*

PRAYERS AT THE OFFERING

Receive, O Lord, these offerings of your people. Remember in your love those who give them and those for whom they have been given, and by your Holy Spirit embody them with power for your purposes.

Some good that we cannot ourselves accomplish we pray that these gifts of our hands may do, our Father. Through them let your Word be spoken, your healing effected, your love made plain.

We put these gifts in the hands of your stewards, Lord. Guard their stewardship, we pray, and let it be in truth a ministry in Jesus' name.

With the gift of our gifts we mean to give you ourselves, our Father. Take then these offerings, we pray, and grant that through them we may work your works where you would have us be.

We give you nothing but what already belongs to you, Lord, since all that we have has come through your grace. Vouchsafe then that these gifts may serve your purposes—be a voice for your word, a hand for your will.

Almighty God, our heavenly Father, you who have freely given us all things, help us through these our own gifts to yield ourselves to you, that with body, mind, and heart we may truly serve you and in your service find our freedom and joy, our strength and peace.

Father of might and of mercy, Giver of all good things, you have taught us that it is more blessed to give than to receive. We offer these gifts as to yourself, and we pledge ourselves in this church to be servants of your will in the world which you so loved that you gave it your Son.

We have sung our praise, Lord, and now we give it. Receive, we pray, these fruits of our work and so transform them by your powerful grace that they may proclaim your name abroad and serve your will afar.

Gold we bring not, our Father, nor frankincense, nor myrrh, but still we come as did those men of old and lay our gifts before you. Receive them, we pray, and let them be tools for your love.

Not wise men, Lord, nor possessed of treasure vast and wonderful, we come no less as if to the manger and lay our gifts before your Son. Grant that they may be the means whereby in humble place and lowly guise he becomes again incarnate, the Word made flesh among us.

We bring our gifts to this your holy house, O Lord, because we dedicate them to a purpose not our own. Let them bear your righteousness beyond these walls, declare your love for all the world, speak peace to every land and nation.

How much we receive and how little we give, our Father. How much we seize and how little we release. Yet the little we bring to your altar we know we ought to bring, and the much that we withhold we want to want to bring. Save us then from the smallness of our hearts, and empower their largeness.

Father almighty, Spirit pure and holy, we wish that our gifts were clean. We wish that they were unblemished, unstained, untainted by the motives we have had in their gathering and the reluctance we have felt in their surrender. Yet better their use in your praise than their hoarding to foster our greed. So we pray that you will so enlighten the minds and kindle the hearts of those who use our offerings that good may be done, if not through our righteousness at least in spite of our sins.

How many times we have been told, our Father, that bringing our gifts to the church, we bring them to you. Yet never have we seen your hands taking the plates at the altar or heard your voice acknowledging that our offerings were now in your keeping. Remind us, we pray, that when of old your Word was made flesh, it dwelt among us in a man named Jesus. Lord, is it not true that still you have no hands but human hands, no voice but that of the people who serve you?

We have so much, Lord, and we give so little. Yet what we give we give in hope that you will guide its use to mighty causes. Let nothing small be done with what we offer here—nothing selfish, nothing unkind.

Work your holy magic on these gifts, we pray, our Father. Let them be the means whereby your Word is spoken, your witness borne, your healing done, your will made plain.

We trust our gifts to human hands, O Lord, but only since we cannot trust them straight to you. Grant then that they who use them in your name may not forget the one to whom they have been given.

Let these gifts remain but briefly on this altar, Lord. Soon may they be flesh for your spirit, agents of your ministry, wings for your Word.

Touch, O God, the hearts and hands of those who will use these gifts in your name, and grant that when you see what they have done, it may be such that you can call it good.

To feed the hungry and clothe the naked, to heal the sick and comfort the afflicted, to give strength to the weak and love to the lonely and hope to the hopeless, we dedicate these gifts, our Father.

Let your kingdom come upon the earth, O God, and by our gifts may we hasten the day of its coming. For to that end have we given, and for that victory we pray.

Our Father and our God, to you who give all, we give thanks for what you give. Touch our hearts with gratitude, we pray, and lead us into ever deeper joy in giving.

God almighty and eternal, you who once were flesh in Jesus Christ, be flesh again in these gifts that we have brought to this church. Let them be feet to run your errands, mouths to speak your words, backs to bear your burdens.

Accept, O Lord, these offerings intended for your praise. Let them sing your glory in the highest, and on the earth may they speed the day of peace among those with whom you are pleased.

Father, Son, and Holy Spirit, God of grace and Lord of glory, grant that our gifts may go before you to prepare your ways among the men and women you have made, to give knowledge of your forgiveness of sins and your salvation to your people, and as your light is shed on those who sit in darkness and in the shadow of death, may their feet be guided into the way of peace.

We have brought our gifts to lay at your feet, O Lord, and we pray that where our treasure is, there our hearts may be also.

Some of us would be priests, our Father, and some would be pastors. Some would declare your truth from pulpits, carry your Word beyond the seas, lead your congregations in their tasks of peace and mercy. But the deeds we wish that we might do many of us cannot. Accept then these offerings to empower those who can, and spurn not our hope that where our gifts may go, a little of ourselves may be.

PRAYERS BEFORE THE SERMON

I shall speak, my Father, and try to speak in your name. Protect me from the blasphemy of confusing prejudice with truth and of fastening on petty preferences the labels of your own holy will. Cleanse my mind of error, my heart of malice, my soul of pride and unworthy desire.

It is not easy, Lord, to speak to many and yet speak to each the word most needed, not easy to speak the word most needed when not sure what needs plead most to be met. Grant now that light may shine on some darkness, balm be laid on some wound, fire be kindled in some gallant resolve.

Lord God, Father of Jesus Christ and our Father, this pulpit is not mine but yours, and so the voice and words should be. Let nothing here be said that does not begin with the gospel of your Son and end in life conforming to your will. Speak to me that I may speak for you. Speak through me that I may speak to those who wait to hear your word.

Small though I am, I would speak of great things, my Father. I would lift up the eyes of this congregation that its members may behold your glory; and beholding, adore; and adoring, bow down; and having bowed down, rise up to obey.

Save me, Lord, from fearing so much my own frailty that I forget your mighty power. Help me to trust your care and providence. Let me speak the words which I believe that you have given me and leave to you results and consequences.

Lord God, Father eternal, infinite Spirit, I would speak from this pulpit as one who speaks from the place of your own abiding—not vaunting myself or pretending knowledge and virtues I do not possess, but trying as best I can to see your people through your own eyes, to love them as you do yourself, and to bring them words that you yourself would have them hear. Accept my offering, I pray, and use me for your purposes.

Because of me or in spite of me, let your will now be done, O God. If I speak truly, confirm what I say in the hearts of your people; if I speak falsely, let it be to them as if I did not speak at all; if I cannot help, grant at least that I may not harm.

Who am I to speak to these people, Lord? So many of them are much wiser than I—kinder, braver, more tender and loving. Yet for these moments the task is in my keeping, and I commit myself to do it as I can. Clear my mind of distractions; warm my heart with compassion; fill my soul with faith in your goodness and power.

Grant discernment to these people, my Father. Let them listen with care to the words that I will speak, and let them choose wisely amongst them. The true let them hug to their hearts and remember, the wrong cast out and forget.

Lend power to my words, O God, for I ask of my hearers more than hearing. Let my voice prompt love and compassion, repentance and forgiveness, courage and commitment.

PRAYERS AFTER THE SERMON

The sayable has now been said, my Father, and now the doable is done. Would that yours had been a better servant in this pulpit, but I pray that you who can use even the wrath of your creatures will find use for my own imperfections. Now send forth this congregation in love and courage. Send it out in faith and hope.

Holy Spirit, everywhere abiding and with us in this holy place, so guide this congregation in the use to be made of the words I have spoken that the wise are held fast and the mistaken cast out. I have preached the gospel according to me. Confirm in this people, I pray, only the gospel.

Eternal God, our heavenly Father, once made flesh in Jesus Christ and searching still for bodies disciplined to serve you, enflesh yourself again, I pray, in the members of this congregation. If there be truth in words that I have spoken, let those words be means whereby you persuade this people to work the works you need of them. Make the hearers doers. Make them eyes and ears for you; make them hands and feet.

Almighty God, great beyond all human imagining, holy past any other's achieving, I have finished my speaking but not ended my duty to the words I have spoken. Help me now to do what I have counseled doing, and grant that in the days to be unfolded before us, the one who has spoken and the ones who have heard may become one body for your particular grace, responsive to your bidding, obedient to your command.

If no sparrow falls without your caring, Lord, neither does one of your children suffer or rejoice, stride in hope or stumble in fear, lose work or find it, find friends or lose them, betray or be faithful, live or die. Be then a presence known to all here gathered, and let some word that I have spoken bring peace, give strength, shed light.

God of all knowledge and wisdom, Lord of all compassion and pity, if in blindness I have not seen the needs of this people, if in deafness not heard their cries for help; if in haste I have blundered or in ignorance wounded; if in folly I have added weight to your burdens or not lightened their load—forgive, I pray. Do by other means what I have failed to do, and let your kingdom come, your will be done.

We bow again to bless your name, our Father, and to seek your Word in the words here spoken. Grant that choosing wisely among them, we may face the coming days with vision cleared and faith renewed.

We are your disciples, Lord, your priests in the priesthood of all who believe. Grant then that in the fellowship of your love we may be more than hearers. Teach us to speak for you, to work for you, to live for you.

So ends the sermon, our Father, and now begins the time of testing. How much have we truly heard? How much have we really believed? How quickly shall we forget, how soon lose hold on our noble intentions? Keep us faithful, we pray. Keep us honest, kind, brave.

We came to this place to seek you, Lord. Some have found and others failed to find, but to all of us you have been a spirit near and caring, a presence ready and waiting. Be with us no less when we leave this house and turn toward our homes; and seeking you still, may still more of us find.

PRAYERS OF BENEDICTION

Touch with your fire, our Father, the worship that we have rendered you this day. Set aflame our noblest aspirations, and help us to become what we ought long since to have been.

Let us not be complacent, our Father. We could have done worse, much worse, than gather in your house at this time. But we can do better, much better, than leave this holy place thinking that we have completed our work for the week as followers of your Son, Christians, members of the church.

So ends our worship. Grant now that as we move to worlds beyond the church's walls, we may be just but not unmerciful, strong but not arrogant, clever but not lacking in wisdom, obedient to fact but not scornful of faith.

As we have worshiped you, our Father, we have wished that we were better than we are—more just and more loyal, more patient and more kind. In the days that wait for us to live them, so lead us, we pray, that we may have the courage of our noblest yearnings, that we may climb a little higher than we believed it possible for us to climb, dig a little deeper.

Lord of all being, Creator, Sustainer, and Redeemer, we have celebrated here the central affirmations of our faith. Now let us not forget, and help us, being a people of faith, to be also a people of truth and righteousness, of love and joy and hope.

We have come, our Father, and now we go. We have met, and now we bid farewell. Yet how can we fare well if we fare not well with you? Grant then that all we do be done as in your sight and by your leading.

Go with us even when we would not go with you, our Father. In sin forgive and in pride confound, in triumph chasten and in defeat renew, in faith keep us humble and in doubt hold us firm. In everything we do alone or together, at work or at play, let all be done as a gift to be laid on your altar.

We go, Lord, but not from you. Grant that when we come again, it may be with some new gift of words spoken in kindness, of deeds done in righteousness and courage.

Go with us, Father, that we may go with you. In weakness make us brave and in strength keep us gentle. In ignorance open our minds to your leading, and in knowledge bend our hearts to your will. We strive to be perfect: perfect us in our striving.

We have lifted our hearts to your glory, Lord. Lure them now, we pray, to your service. Teach us to care for those for whom the world could not care less. Nurture us in friendship, peace, and sacrifice. Offer us a cross, and strengthen us to bear it.

As we have worshiped you here, our Father, others have worshiped you in other ways and other places. Let us not forget our brothers and our sisters in the faith. In the streets and in the offices, in the schools and on the playing fields, in the stores and in the hospitals, grant us to link our arms with them and march in common step toward ends that have no end save the love we bear for you and all that you have made.

Before we leave this house devoted to your praise, once more we open our hearts to your spirit, our Father. Hear us, we pray. Hear us, and grant that the sins here confessed may be forgiven and done no more; that the hopes here encouraged may be cleansed and fulfilled; and that the commitments here made in the name of your Son may be confirmed and made flesh.

From this house of prayer and praise we return, our Father, to our homes and apartments, our lonely rooms and motels. Let us not be blind to our husbands, our wives, and our children; not deaf to our brothers and sisters; not inattentive to our friends, our neighbors, and even our casual acquaintances. Caring for you, we would not be careless of them. Loving you, we strive to love what you have made.

Lord, our worship nears its end, and from this house set apart to your glory we turn again toward home. Let not the aspirations of this hour be left behind us as we go, and grant that having worshiped you in word, we may worship you no less in deed.

We have remembered you in worship, Lord. Let us not forget you in play and in work. We have gathered, and now we part; and we pray that in the days before we meet again, we may not be faithless to one another or to you.

You have been with us in worship, our Father. Be with us now as worship ends. Strengthen us when we serve you. Weaken us when we thwart you. Forgive us when in weakness or in strength we fall short of our high calling in Jesus Christ.

There is peace in this place, our Father, and we would take that peace through all the coming days. There is power in this place, and we would feel that power when we need it most. There is truth in this place, and we would stand upon that truth and never be dismayed. So be it, Lord. So be it.

So the service ends, our Father, and with it once again the worship that we offer each week to you, our Creator and Lord. As members of this church, we have gathered here to praise you who made the worlds and all that is in them, to call to mind again that we are souls whose bodies are but incidental to the life that they were truly meant to live, and to seek your will for us. In the hours yet remaining to us in the days that stretch before us, week on busy week, we pledge ourselves to do your will with faithfulness. So we pause a moment now, and in the quietness we tell you again how much we love and want to serve you, how weak we are and much we need you; and each as each has the will and all as all have the way, we open our hearts to you and ask you to make them clean, to make them calm, to make them strong.

Father almighty, Spirit high and holy, always we struggle to think your thoughts after you, and always we are after you. We thank you for what we have seen; we thank you for your patience with us in what we might have seen but would not; and most of all we thank you for so revealing yourself to us in Jesus Christ that in our blindness we still see you, that in our ignorance we still know you, and that in our sin we still receive your love.

PRAYERS FOR THE ORDINANCES AND SACRAMENTS

Baptism/Dedication

For a Child

Holy Spirit, eternal Father, you embrace each person on earth as one of your children. We ask for your particular remembrance of this little one brought here for your blessing. How wonderful the birth of a baby; how difficult the rearing of a child! All the more earnestly then we pray that these parents may be led by you so to live that their son may be led by them to yourself. In them may he ever find truth, patience, kindness, hope. Through them may he learn to love and not count the cost, to give and not demand reward, to serve and not expect acclaim. As he increases in wisdom and strength, so may he grow too in awareness of your sustaining and chastening presence in his daily endeavors and become one day a faithful disciple of your Son, Jesus Christ, in whose name we pray. *Amen.*

Most holy and merciful God, Father never begotten but begetting all of your people as children, we bring to this house of prayer a child beloved of her parents and offered to you for your blessing. How small she is, how weak, how readily unnoticed in the turmoil and tumult of the world wherein her life is now set! Still, you called her by name before she was born, and in your love she owns a place that none but herself can fill. Kindle in her parents fresh awareness of the holy gift now charged to their keeping. Fill them with awe before the magnitude of their responsibility for a being so precious in your sight and so fruitful with hope for all who will know her. Save them from ignorance in their providing, impatience in their insisting, carelessness in their caring. Surrounded by friends and loved ones, aided by doctors and teachers, and ever enlivened by your favorful grace, may this little girl, now helpless, emerge at last in womanhood, strong to share the joys, endure the sorrows, bear the burdens, and win the victories of all who pledge themselves disciples of your Son, Jesus Christ. Hear our petition, we pray. Hear, and answer as best will further your will and your kingdom. In Jesus' name. *Amen.*

PRAYERS FOR ALL OCCASIONS

For an Adult

Creator, Father, Redeemer, ever of old you have summoned your people to serve you, and always some have heard and obeyed. We here present to you a man who offers himself to be one of your ministers, laboring for you through labor with his brothers and sisters in the work of the world beyond the church's borders. Into this priesthood of all believers he has now been admitted in the ancient sacrament of baptism, and we pray for your blessing on what we have done in your name.

Today, Lord, he stands at the start of his journey, an enlisted disciple of Jesus; where will he be at its end? Grant that when he has finished his course, he may have kept the faith, that he may not have been gotten by the things he has got, that he may harbor for no one any wish but goodwill, that his mind may be clear and his heart warm and his soul untwisted by guilt or by fear. Let him do with diligence the tasks by which he earns his daily bread and be in the place of his working himself an outpost of the heavenly kingdom. Let him so live in his home that his life proclaims your presence and becomes to those nearest and dearest an anchor, a shelter, a light. Let him receive to himself the full allotment of his burdens in the church and be among his fellow disciples a toiler dependable and stalwart. Manifest yourself in him, our Father; manifest yourself through him; manifest yourself in spite of him. Through Jesus Christ our Lord. *Amen.*

Almighty God, Eternal Father, in Jesus Christ once incarnate and through your Holy Spirit ever present in the midst of your people, we have presumed to act for you in this holy sacrament of baptism, and we pray that you will enliven the words we have spoken and empower the deeds we have done.

We intend the act here performed to be the act of a new beginning, and as this woman enters the church of your Son, we beg your blessing on the life she undertakes. Christian by profession, may she be Christlike in practice. A minister in the ministering community of all pledged and accepted disciples, may she exercise her ministry ever in true faith and hearty allegiance. Wherever she goes, let her go as bent on your errand; whatever she does, let her do as done in your sight. Shield her from prejudice and hatred, from envy and fear and despair. Allow her conscience no sleep when she thinks of the friendless and the lonely, the poor and the homeless, the tempted and the frightened. Thrust back her every horizon, and from the scope of her loving concern let no nation or people be lost or excluded.

Keep sweet within her the springs that nourish her soul, O Lord; build strong the faith that steadies her step. Afflicted, may she not be crushed; perplexed, not left hopeless; persecuted, not abandoned; struck down, not destroyed. Enable her so to use the talents which you have bestowed upon her that others may see her good works and be led by her to praise and obey you. Endue her so with your grace that in peace and loving-kindness she may be a worthy agent of your righteousness and mercy. And yours be the kingdom and the power and the glory, world without end. *Amen.*

The Lord's Supper

Almighty God, Father of Jesus Christ and our Father, Holy Spirit dwelling ever in our midst, how humble you are in your majesty, how unassuming in your approaches to the lowly! Incarnate once in the carpenter's son of Nazareth, stable-born and village-raised, in life at home among the dispossessed and in death a companion of thieves on the cross—how meek you were in your surest revealing, how quiet in the signs of your presence and purpose! Be known of us now, we pray, in the bread and the cup. Consuming these elements, may we partake indeed of yourself, so entering our bodies that you take command of our minds and our hearts. Yours by creation, we would also be yours in commitment and service. In Jesus' name. *Amen.*

Let your blessing rest upon this bread and cup, our Father. Prepare us to receive them as indeed from the hands of your Son, and grant that remembering his death to save sinners no worse than ourselves, we sin ourselves no more but stand firm henceforth in faith and allegiance. *Amen*

Render holy to us in full truth this sacrament of holy Communion, our Father. Free us from all distractions of means and of method. Blind us to those who serve and to those who wait to be served. Deafen us to sounds that rise from the pews or slip in from the doors and the windows. Fasten our minds to the bread and the cup, and in them let us find only your Son, laying down his life for our sakes and redeeming us still from our sins. For we pray in his name. *Amen.*

Bless this bread and this cup, O Lord. Let them be heralds of peace, tidings of hope, and bearers of love to all who believe. *Amen.*

God of all power and knowledge, Lord of all goodness and grace, again we gather at the table of your Son, and again we understand but in part the reasons for our gathering. So often we have come without purpose and left without achievement. So often the bread and the cup have seemed no more than empty symbols of an even greater emptiness. Yct still the holy table draws us to itself; and we pray that in these common things of taste and touch you will manifest yourself anew, forgive us those sins of which our consciences are afraid, and so fill us with your spirit that henceforth we may have in us that mind which was also in Christ Jesus our Lord. *Amen.*

Holy Spirit, heavenly Father, beyond whom nothing is and without whom nothing would have been, so easily we speak the words that so swiftly have no meaning: "This is my body; this is my blood." But has your Son been truly with us in these moments? Have we known him indeed in our hearts? Have we so partaken of these common things of earth that partaking of them, we have partaken of him? From the sheltered quiet of these walls we turn to face the world again, and we pray that you will make these moments burrs to stick upon us and never loosc their hold—sometimes scarlet letters reminding us of sins we should like to forget, sometimes badges of faith enlightening and sustaining us. We would remember Jesus. We would remember and follow. *Amen.*

Almighty and most merciful God, we meet again in your presence before the mystery of your Son, and we set apart these common elements to be uncommon. Forgive, we pray, the sins that have brought us to this hour unprepared for its glory. Forgive the wanderings of mind and the coldness of heart that keep us from its chastening pain and enlivening hope. If it be possible, breach now the wall between us and yourself, and grant that we may gratefully receive your gift for our sakes, through Jesus Christ our Lord. *Amen.*

So ends the sacrament, our Father; and we praise you, we thank you, and we bless your holy name that you have sent your light to shine in our darkness and to lead us through the days still left to us on earth. So much of our time has been wasted, so much spent in exalting ourselves, so much spent in pretending a goodness that could not support its pretenses, so much spent in fleeing the grace that sought only the chance to be gracious. All the more then do we praise you, thank you, and bless your holy name that once again in this place you have revealed yourself to us in Jesus Christ; and we pray that going forth, we may go forward—unsure but sure enough to know the next step to be taken, weak but not too weak to carry any burden other than our own, troubled but fearful less that you will fail us than that we may fail you. *Amen.*

Ordination

God of all the ages that have been and are and yet shall come to be, Maker of earth and Father of all people, Lord of truth and of justice, of love and of mercy, less to do a deed have we come to this place than to celebrate a deed already done. If you have not long since laid holy hands upon this man, no hands of ours can make him holy. If long ago this congregation was not gathered at your call and summons, small chance there is that you will here transform a coterie to be a church or bestow upon an audience the powers of a royal priesthood. And if yours was not the will that brought this pastor to this people, today we seek in vain your blessing on this union. So we come to this hour in faith that we come at your bidding; and hailing the grace now granted so richly, we offer you discipleship, and we open our hearts to the chastening gifts of your spirit.

Far better than ourselves you know the needs of your people here assembled, but with some of them we have wrestled almost to despair. How weak we are where most we ought to be strong! How blind where most we ought to see! How full of hatred where most we ought to love! Pledged to serve, we seek only to be comfortable; calling a minister, we want only to be ministered unto; and praising the cross, we search for someone else to bear it.

Save this union of pastor and people, our Father. Save us, for we cannot save ourselves. Save us from the tired old formalities and the deadly old routines that keep the conscience happy beneath polite and decent profanation. Let not this people make life easy for its pastor, but let the burdens that it lays upon him be the burdens of your kingdom. Vouchsafe to him who leads this congregation the bravery to speak in duty to his lonely vision, but grant him, too, an ear for prophecy among the led. We pray for the souls of this pastor and people, that their sins may be discovered, repented, and forgiven. We pray for their minds, that there be no clouding of the facts and the truth in their deliberations and conclusions. We pray for their hearts, that hurt to others may be hurt to themselves and that justice may ever open doors to compassion. But most of all we pray for their wills, O Lord; for the good that we would exceeds so vastly the good that we do. So it is the deed toward which we pray that you will prod us: righteousness here; love now; the second mile; the other cheek; the laying down of life for a friend here and now, in this place, this congregation, this pastor, and people. Through Jesus Christ our Lord. *Amen.*

Holy Spirit, Creator and Friend, who so loved the world as to give it your Son and so loved your Son as to leave for him in the church a new body to live in the world of your loving, we have gathered in this place set apart for Christian ministry to celebrate your setting apart of a woman to be a Christian minister. On this day, at this hour, and in this house of sacred meeting, we declare to all afar and near that you have summoned this woman to your particular service, and in the company of your chosen disciples we commission her to march among those at the head.

When she preaches, grant that she may ever preach not words but the Word. When she handles human souls, let her mind be kept warm by compassion and her heart held firm in the truth. When she leads her congregation in your praise, guard her from such anxiety about leading that she overlooks her need to be praising. To her people let her be as coach to playing team, general to fighting army, maestro to performing orchestra, minister to ministering community. Enable her so to see and so to hear, so to think and so to pray, so to speak and so to act, so to enlighten and so to inspire that wherever any member of her church is found, there, too, will be an agent of your will.

Now, Lord, we lay upon the head of this woman the hands that represent the ancient lineage of your apostles. To her we entrust the sacraments and special tasks of Christian ministry; upon her we rest their burdens, and for her we covet their joys. Well blessed in past days when she moved within the shelter of those who surrounded and sustained her, may she be blessed as surely now while called and commissioned. Prepared and committed, she makes her own professions, claims her own vocation, and assumes her own responsibilities. In strength keep her humble and in weakness undiscouraged. Shield her from loneliness; save her from fear; protect her from the need to be protected. When the end of her days at last is upon her, let it be said and said truly that she fought the good fight, that she finished her course, and that she kept the faith. So be it, Lord. With your help so be it. In Jesus' name. *Amen.*

Gracious God, in whom alone dwells the fulness of wisdom and goodness, who existed before the worlds began and who will still exist when the worlds are no more, we thank you for your presence on the earth today. Creator of old, you still create. Lover of your people in the years that are gone, now you love them none the less. As your word was ever sent to call your chosen, so the hour strikes again when you summon one of your children to be one of your ministers. We bless you, our Father. We magnify your holy name.

Accept now, we pray, the offering of him who kneels before you in this holy place. You know how he longs to serve you in a ministry unburdened by his sins and weaknesses. You know how he shares with all of us the need of your forgiveness, the need of your love, the need of your power. Therefore we beseech you to do for him what man can never do for anyone: to see him clear and see him whole, to separate his talents from his incapacities, and to lead him to that point of labor where the utmost of his strength can meet the direst of your pain.

Give him doubt enough about himself to have no doubt about his need of you, but also give him faith enough in you to have no doubt about your need of him. Make him confident, but not arrogant; humble, but not obsequious; just, but not unmerciful; sympathetic, but not soft; shrewd, but not unscrupulous. Let him be your prophet, and when he speaks for you, save him from confusing your words with his own. Let him be your priest, and when he leads a congregation toward the throne of grace, save him from standing between your people and yourself. Let him be your shepherd, and when he finds a flock entrusted to his care, save him from feeding on the sheep that needed to be fed.

In your name we place our hands upon him, and we set him apart from his fellows that he may be to them strength in their weakness, peace in their strife, light in their darkness, hope in their sorrow. Him whom you have called we ordain to his calling, and him whom you have charged with faith we charge to be faithful. Through Jesus Christ our Lord. *Amen.*

Eternal God, who were before anyone knew you, who are though many deny you, and who still will be when all have died who now still live, we gather in this place to set apart for your service a woman whose will is not to serve you in a place kept apart. Ever of old you have summoned your chosen to be servants of your servants, and never have your people needed more than now the ministry of those who give their lives to be your ministers. Therefore do we praise you most heartily that you have led this woman to affirm herself through self-denial for your sake; and we assemble here to acknowledge, to celebrate, and to make visible among all of your people this newest wonder of your wondrous love for humankind.

We pray for your church, that it may accept with gratitude your gift of her who will equip it for its ministry. Grant that it may fail her neither by demanding of her too much nor by expecting of her too little. Let it find in her the earnest of that calling to which your church itself is called; and taught by her as she is taught by you, may it discover in its heritage both the cause to be humble and the warrant to be brave.

But praying urgently for your church, we pray with even greater urgency for this your church's servant who, kneeling in the presence of this congregation, kneels not to this people but to you; and now as we lay our hands upon her head, we beseech you that this act may be no idle gesture, one more mockery in that endless parade of betrayals by which your church has often pretended faithfulness it neither possessed nor wanted to possess. Surround this woman with your love, our Father; fill her with your spirit; ordain her with your power. Vouchsafe that henceforth she may never stand alone nor think that she so stands, and assured by your nearness, may she also be chastened. In fear make her stalwart and in doubt, undismayed; in temptation keep her steadfast and in failure, unembittered; and let her diligence in study, prayer, and labor so enrich and enable her ministry that she may bless her people evermore. Through Jesus Christ our Lord. *Amen.*

Marriage

Almighty God, eternal Father, Holy Spirit of love and compassion, ever in your presence, we rejoice in your particular nearness as we celebrate the union of this man and this woman. It is a holy thing that we undertake in this place. Was it not you who created us male and female? Did you not yourself ordain the family to be the soil wherein would grow and prosper the creatures whom you had begotten? Have you any means but human to nurture little ones in the way they should go? It is a holy thing we undertake in this place, O Lord, and we covet your aid and approval. Surround us then with your care, we pray, and sustain and uplift us; and grant that when this service is ended, we may have done a good deed in your sight. Through Jesus Christ our Lord. *Amen.*

Love divine, all other loves excelling, we bring before you in this house designed for your praise two lives that long to be joined in a bond that merits your blessing. On different paths they have approached this point of their merging, and each brings memories the other knows not. Each in your sight is a person distinct, and each stands alone in your judgment and calling. Yet both now are soon to be one, and we pray that their oneness may be one of your hallowing. In what they do here, help them to be aware of you. Stir in their hearts the will to respond and henceforward obey. Through Jesus Christ our Lord. *Amen.*

God of the ages, Lord of this moment, by whose will the worlds were created and in whose love all people live and have their being, hear our prayer as we seek your blessing for this man and this woman. Far better than we could ever know them you have long known them yourself, and no secrets from you are their hopes and their dreams, their joys and their sorrows, their successes and their failures. Look upon them now with compassion and favor, we pray, and bestow upon them the benediction of your grace as, no longer two, they set out to be one.

Let them not stumble before they start, expect bliss at a snap or a whistle, demand as a gift what has to be earned. Teach them to foresee disagreements and be prepared to handle them with restraint and forbearance. However hurried and harried their days may prove, let none be so crowded with haste that they have no time for each other, no time for listening, touching, caring. Deny them the folly of taking each other for granted, looking at each other but never really seeing, hearing each other but never actually comprehending. Dissuade them from prolonging quarrels, nursing grudges, entrenching themselves in surly silences. May every night wipe clean the slate of their grievances and every morning open doors to renewal and joy.

Will it not be good, our Father, if this man and woman make your love a pattern for their own? Will it not be victory for them and all humankind if their love is patient and tender, not jealous or boastful, not arrogant or rude; if it does not insist on its own way, is not irritable or resentful, does not rejoice at wrong but rejoices in the right; if it bears all things, believes all things, hopes all things, endures all things? As you create all, grant that this man and this woman may partake with you in your creation, and when their days on earth are ended, may their labors have been such that with all your good and faithful servants they enter the joy of their Lord. In Jesus' name. *Amen.*

Gracious God, our heavenly Father, our Holy Spirit, our sovereign Lord, we have come to this house of prayer to pray for this man and this woman and to solemnize with them in your presence the vows that they make to each other. Grant that they may not treat lightly the promises here made nor fail to understand their consequence. To love another human being for better for worse, for richer for poorer, in sickness and in health till death compels a parting—how stupendous a pledge; how incredible the trust and commitment of anyone who undertakes to perform it; how impossible the task if you are not present to uplift and sustain! So we commend this man and woman to your keeping and pray that you will strengthen them henceforth to fulfill the covenant now entered.

Maintain in them always the glory they knew at the dawn of their loving. Defend them from obsession with buying and selling. Intrigue them more strongly with homes than with houses. Both faulty themselves, let neither be surprised by faults in the other; and each needing forgiveness, let each be quick to forgive. They will be polite with acquaintances, kind with neighbors, generous with friends, and amicable with colleagues and business associates; grant that they may be no less with themselves. As neither should be slave, let neither be tyrant. As each needs the faith of the other, may neither be unfaithful.

We pray for this new home, our Father, that it may be fastened to truth, filled with compassion, enlivened by hope, and dedicated to sharing with you the redemption of the world which you so loved that you gave it your Son. Hear our prayer, we beseech you; hear and answer in accordance with your wisdom and mercy. Through Jesus Christ our Lord. *Amen.*

Funeral

The best funeral and memorial prayers are inescapably personal in their detail and reference, and it is not possible to provide such prayers for one person that will be equally appropriate for all. The first two prayers in this section are complete and were actually used in services. The others are meant to suggest a framework to which specific items may be added.

God of all power and truth, Father of all goodness and love, eternal Spirit whose cogent mercy dwells ever among us yet always beyond, hear our prayer as we come before you in the name of [name].

How sorely we miss him, Lord, as we walk where he walked, sit where he sat, bear the burdens borne so long upon the shoulders now withdrawn from us. Was he too steadily kind, too patient, too just, too good, so that words and deeds that would have been in other men rare pearls and priceless came from him in such abundance that being constant, they appeared to be common? Did we build upon the walls he built and not discern the Builder of the rock he built upon? Did we take him too much for granted, like the air we breathe and the water we drink, and is it not until now and too late that we know the words to tell him what he meant to us?

We remember [name], our Father, and shall remember him as long as life is given us for living: the gentleman and gentle man, gracious in manner and manners, ever being what we wanted to be ourselves but were not. We remember [name], our Father, and shall remember him however far the tides and times may sweep us from the places where we knew him: the preacher whose word was the Word, the pastor who fed his sheep and did not feed upon them, the teacher who might have taught without teaching because already he had taught by what he had become. We remember [name]: the compassionate man from whose great heart no pain or need was turned roughly away, the radiant man whose very countenance sang songs of trust and faith and joy, the man of all places and peoples in whose embracing mind no land was foreign nor any person not a kinsman.

For all he was and is and is to be we praise you. For all the lives that touching his were transformed in the touching we thank you. For all the hours that are brighter because of him, for all the roads that are straighter because of him, for all the dreams that are nobler because of him we bless your holy name. And praying for your strong and tender care of her he held most dear, we turn to the tasks of our separate callings, many in body but one in gratitude that [name] lived and that he lived where we could know and love him. Through Jesus Christ our Lord. *Amen.*

Father of all people, Maker of no one to be a copy of anyone else and Lover of each as if he were your only child, we thank you for your son [name] and for all in him that met with favor in your sight.

So much of him was known to so few, and we praise you for the tender memories of him that linger in the hearts of those who knew him best, praying that she to whom he was husband and they to whom he was father may find in those memories the strength that loss cannot diminish and the love that death cannot destroy. But so much of him, too, was known to so many, and we thank you for the life he lived among us in his daily work and recreation. For the gruffness of manner that often hid a softness of heart, for the skill with tools that made him a workman needing not to be ashamed, for the closeness to the earth that marked him as a partner with yourself in the garden he cherished, for the yearly adoption of daughters that endlessly multiplied the girls whom he served as a father, for the silent acceptance of the illness that left him no hour without death at his elbow—for these and all things else that were his offerings to this place and this people we lift our souls to you in gratitude.

Sad that he died so soon, we yet rejoice that he was spared long confinement to a bed that would have been for him a prison house of restless agony. Death came swiftly, and we are glad; the hand of death was peace, and we are grateful. But now we pray that you will be no less gentle with the family upon whose hearts the burden of his loss has been so quickly laid. Confirm in them their faith in you and in your providence for all the people you have made to be your children. Renew in them their knowledge of your Son, who lived and died and rose to live forevermore in witness of the life that earth cannot contain. Let your Holy Spirit so abide with them that in their weakness they find strength, in their darkness they see light, and in their bereavement they discover hope. Through Jesus Christ our Lord. *Amen.*

You know, our Father, with what conflicting emotions we stand beside this grave: sad, but wishing that we could be sadder; relieved, but still guilty about our relief; believing, but yet not wholly free from doubt. Let not our hearts be troubled beyond the point of benefit. All that we could do for this woman has now been done, and the tree is barren that seeks its sustenance in that which might have been. Help us to let go. Help us to rise up and be faithful. In Jesus' name. *Amen.*

God, Father, Holy Spirit, once more now we pause at the last, turn toward you and affirm our faith in your powerful care. To the ground we commit only the body of this man whom we have loved. Himself we commend to your tender providence, trusting that if we die in Christ, we rise too with him in newness of life; for we pray in his name. *Amen.*

Almighty and eternal God, not like those who have no faith do we turn to you now, nor as those who see no road beyond the hour when you take from them one deeply loved, nor after the manner of people broken and afraid and hopeless. We turn to you, rather, in sober thanksgiving; and thinking of this woman whom we have cherished, we give you thanks for all that we have known of her. To us she was a witness of your love; and losing her awhile, we do not rebuke you for her passing from us, nor do we question your goodness in our deprivation. We pray that in these moments spent together in this holy place of worship, our minds may be quieted, our hearts healed, and our souls so taught to rest in you that henceforth we shall walk in faithfulness and peace the road in which you lead us. Through Jesus Christ our Lord. *Amen.*

Holy God, our heavenly Father, whose life is with this moment and yet with ages more than we can ever know, whose ways are with this world but still with worlds beyond our farthest sight, in these minutes of calm we leave the pressures of the day behind, and we turn our thoughts to you and you alone. We thank you that in the mysteries of birth and death you invade our complacent existence and summon us to pause and consider. We thank you that you compel us to think of that which eye has not seen and ear has not heard, and we thank you that through Christ you have given us the witness of a life that does not end. Grant now that gathered here in memory of one we knew of old, we may keep channels open to receive from you the benediction of your light and peace. In Jesus' name. *Amen.*

How swiftly, our Father, you have taken from us one whom we have dearly loved. How suddenly removed from us the very ground on which we seemed to stand. But yesterday this man was here among us, and now he walks with us no more and shall not be with us on the earth again. You know well how much we cared for him, how much we rested on his strength, how much we needed him; and now that he is gone, we come before you stunned and broken. Emptied of its cherished meaning, life lies now before us as a thing almost unwanted, and if you do not lift us up and lead us on, we shall be forever fallen, forever hopeless, forever lost. So abide with us in this hour, we pray, and through the days ahead be in us the strength we do not have ourselves.

We bless you even now for what this man has meant to us through the years of his life in our midst: his integrity and good judgment, his kindness, loyalty, and faith. That we could know him, that we could live by his side, that so many years were granted us for fellowship and love—these things are precious to us, Lord; and even as we ask why you took him from us now, we thank you that you let us know him at all. Be with him today and always as you have since first you gave him his being. He will be restless if you do not give him work to do and lonely if you do not assure him that we love him still. We would that we might meet his need as once of old we did, but since he dwells beyond our present reach, be yourself to him what we would be and more, that he may be at peace and find new joy while parted trails move toward their destined meeting.

Upon the earth you still have paucity of willing hands, O Lord. There are so few to hear your word and heed, so few to put your will above their own and serve others more than self. Teach us then to seek no more than need be for answers which must still be hidden from our mortal eyes; and trusting where we cannot clearly see, may we be led to serve you here on earth. Save us from despair; save us from self-pity; save us from the frailty of those who have no knowledge of your love. And grant that we may soon be found again among the workers—heads held high and hearts illumined, looking toward the day when we shall meet again this man from whom we now are severed. Until that day may we be sustained by faith that you still have a place for us on earth and still pledge power for the tasks with which we are commissioned. Through Jesus Christ our Lord. *Amen.*

Lord of the ages, King of creation, Father of our spirits, we struggle toward your presence, and in the hidden depths of heart and soul we seek to know you, to understand you, to trust you. You comprehend our sorrows; you look with tenderness upon the lingerings of doubt and fear. Grant then that in this time of need our doors may open at your bidding. Use these fleeting moments here to reach our hearts and claim them for your own. Heal our souls, that out of sadness may come the joy that conquers tears and out of darkness light that turns the midnight into noonday. Lord, we believe in you; help our unbelief. Through Jesus Christ our Lord. *Amen.*

Eternal and merciful Father, whose eye is on the sparrow's flight and who love even lilies of the field, we call your name and pray that you will manifest yourself to us. You have taken from us one whom we have dearly loved, and though we could not wish her longer in our midst to bear infirmities of body or of mind, we yet cannot dismiss her from our thought as if she had not been. Be known of us this hour, we pray. Deepen our faith in your providence; persuade us that behind the passing of the one we loved was still the steady presence of your wisdom; and through the days to come and go, vouchsafe that we may surely trust your goodness and your power. What once you created and we have cherished long you will not scorn nor cast aside. Lead us then to leave with you the one whom we can guard no more, and for her sake and in her name take up again the tasks of earth. Through Jesus Christ our Lord. *Amen.*

Almighty God, Lord of all worlds and all peoples, we come to you and pray that in the time of need you will be to us as rock on which our feet may surely take their stand. Always we think ourselves prepared, but always in the awful hour it seems we never were prepared at all. So we turn to you and ask that in your mercy you will steady, empower, and lead us.

Speak to us in these moments of quiet. Through the turbulent storms of our sorrow, in the ache of the heart, and in the numbness of the mind, speak to us in a still small voice that still can make us hear. Calm our fevered wills. Enliven our fainting spirits. Open our blinded eyes; unstop our deafened ears; and silencing the thunder of despair, bring us word to send us upward on the road to strength and hope. And yours be the glory forever. *Amen.*

Patient God, caring Father, always present Spirit, how abruptly we have lost this woman whom so profoundly we cherished. In mind we knew that one day we must travel on alone; in heart we were not ready for the loneliness of staying here without her. We think about the years that stretch behind us—the day when first we met the one whom still we love so dearly; the time of courtship and the coming to marriage; the comradeship together on the winding trails of happiness and sorrow. We think about the life of her who came to mean so much to us—her devotion to her husband and her family; her pride in her home; her fascination with the birds of the air and the flowers of the field, with all that flew and all that grew and all that added beauty to a world not always beautiful; her openness of mind and her friendliness of heart; her capacity for thrusting herself through the edges of truth to come with breathless quickness to its hearty center; her restlessness with anything that had neither meaning nor purpose; and her ever widening interests, ever helping her to be more helpful to her fellow human beings.

There is a shadow on these winding trails today, our Father, for now in one sense they have reached their end, and we pray that as we wander backward through that shadow, you will take our hand and be our teacher. We cannot ask that you will spare us pain in losing one whom we have loved so deeply and so long, and we know that days must come before we find again the peace that once we knew. But do not let us linger longer than we should with eyes upon the backward way, O Lord; and as the weeks go by, lead us more and more to fix our minds upon the road ahead. Lodge fast in us the precious memories, and vouchsafe that they may prompt in us henceforth a steadier faith and nobler life. Confident that you are love and love alone, may we conquer fear about the fate of her from whom we have awhile been severed. She is in your keeping. She is in your care. And safe from hurt and free from harm, she is as we would have her be.

So be it, our Father. So be it now and evermore. So be it both for her and for ourselves; and yours be the kingdom and the power and the glory, world without end. *Amen.*